How To Dump A Guy

{A COWARD'S MANUAL}

HOW TO DUMP A GUY

by KATE FILLION *and*
ELLEN LADOWSKY

WORKMAN PUBLISHING

NEW YORK

LIBRARY OF CONGRESS CATALOGING-IN-PUBLICATION DATA
Fillion, Kate.
How to dump a guy : a coward's manual / Kate Fillion and
Ellen Ladowsky.
p.   cm.
Includes index.
ISBN 0-7611-1256-1
1. Man-woman relationships.   2. Separation (Psychology)
3. Single women—Psychology.   4. Man-woman
relationships—Humor.   5. Separation (Psychology)—
Humor.   6. Single woman—Humor.
I. Ladowsky, Ellen, 1964–.   II. Title.
HQ801.F55   1998
646.7'7—dc21   97-52280
                                                       CIP

Workman books are available at special discounts
when purchased in bulk for premiums and sales
promotions as well as for fund-raising or educational use.
Special editions or book excerpts can also be created to
specification. For details, please contact the Special Sales
Director at the address below.

Workman Publishing Company, Inc.
708 Broadway
New York, New York 10003-9555

Manufactured in the United States of America

First Printing April 1998

10 9 8 7 6 5 4 3 2 1

To vintners everywhere

CONTENTS

INTRODUCTION

I t doesn't matter whether you've dated him only once or whether you've been with him for years—if you're like most women, the mere thought of having to dump a guy makes you cringe. In fact, it's such an unappetizing prospect that you can't quite bring yourself to do it. So instead of ditching him, you decide to procrastinate for a few more weeks. Or months.

This pattern of behavior is all too familiar to us. Collectively, we have thirty years' experience slithering out of relationships in a most undignified fashion. For a long time, we believed there was only one possible explanation for our behavior: an improper upbringing. But then it dawned on us: perhaps our problem was not a lack of character, but a lack of reading material.

After all, there is a shocking dearth of information on how to dump guys. Although dozens of books cover the finer points of snaring and keeping men, very few have tackled the delicate subject of romantic disposal. The assumption seems to be that ditching a guy is simple—all you have to do is tell him that you don't want to see him again—and that the way you do it is of no import, since it's always going to be unpleasant.

Nothing could be further from the truth. Breaking up is a very complicated business, and, as we discovered after interviewing scores of women, there *is* a way to do it that reduces the pain for both parties. It doesn't matter how cowardly you are—if you're prepared to apply yourself, you too can master the subtle art of dumping a guy.[1]

---

[1]Caution: The tone of the following pages may initially strike some as a little too high-spirited, given the gravity of the subject matter. But learning to view your breakup as something other than a source of angst—namely, as a rich source of hilarity—is actually quite therapeutic. It gives you the perspective and distance you need to go through with the ditch and get on with your life. Besides, we thought it would be a crashing bore to slog through page after page of earnest analysis and preachy advice. Breaking up is unpleasant enough as it is.

HOW TO DUMP A GUY

CHAPTER ONE

How to Know When to Go

S ome women know exactly when the time has come to dump a guy. "I was standing at the kitchen counter and Colin came up behind me, put his arms around my waist, and said in a baby voice, 'Honey, will you make me a sammy? Pwease?' It was nauseating," Susan remembers. "I thought, 'my God, I have to ditch him right away.'"

Sadly, few of us are gifted with Susan's insight —or decisiveness. Instead of taking swift action, we waffle, second-guess ourselves, and bore our friends to tears by repeating the same inane phrase: "If only there were some way to know for sure . . ."

Well, there isn't. And unfortunately, dumping a guy is a highly personal decision. No one else can make it for you. There are, however, some pretty clear indicators that it's time to bolt.

OPINION POLLING

You're running around canvassing friends, family, and virtual strangers: *What do you think I should do?* You're either hoping for confirmation that you should leave, or hoping to be persuaded that you should stay. Either way, every taxi driver and bartender in a thirty-mile radius is conversant with the most intimate details of your relationship.

ZERO TOLERANCE

His mannerisms—the way he sips his coffee, the tone of voice he uses with telemarketers, the way he breathes—irritate you beyond belief. When you're not seething internally, you're lashing out. "One morning, my boyfriend's pant leg was caught in his sock and I went wild, like he'd committed murder or something," remembers Cheryl. In other words, his most innocent actions—things that wouldn't bother you a bit if anyone else did them—seem to be part of a cunningly designed master plan to drive you crazy.

GIVING HIM A MAKEOVER

You're desperate to change everything about him, and to that end, you appoint yourself his full-time voice coach, etiquette instructor, and wardrobe consultant—"I threw out your glasses this morning. I decided you look better in contacts." In fact, you're thinking of giving up your paying job so that you'll have more time to work with him.

TRYING TOO HARD
TO MAKE YOURSELF CARE FOR HIM

You continually tell yourself either "I'm probably just being too picky," or, "But he's such a nice guy, I *ought* to be crazy about him. I'm sure if I really, really try . . . "

TRYING TOO HARD
TO MAKE HIM CARE FOR YOU

You spend every waking moment wondering how he feels about you. You're so obsessed with trying to keep him interested that it never occurs to you to ask yourself whether *you're* actually happy with *him*. You're constantly buying him little gifts, wracking your brain to think of scintillating things to say, and spending your entire paycheck on frisky little outfits. In short, you never let yourself relax in his company.

CONSULTING A
HIGHER AUTHORITY

You have visited a psychic, astrologist, channeler and/or palm reader in your quest for relationship advice. On one occasion, one of us (Ellen, to be precise, who is normally the most skeptical of women when it comes to the spirit world) paid a huge sum to see a charlatan by the name of Mrs. Rosa. Ellen presented a photograph of her boyfriend and begged for supernatural guidance. After pocketing the cash and making a big production of shuffling some tarot cards around, Mrs. Rosa told her, "My guides are telling me that you have trouble making decisions, and you're very bad with money."

TUNING OUT

While he's having what he believes to be a serious conversation with you, you're in a reverie, wondering whether blonde highlights or a subtle henna would suit you better. Time and again his mouth opens, and your mind wanders. "I just couldn't seem to pay attention to Jerry," Leah remembers. "He'd ask me questions and I'd have no idea how to answer, since I hadn't heard a word he'd said."

[*QUIZ ONE*]

You've only dated the guy a few times,
and you're wondering

SHOULD I BE GETTING SERIOUS
—*or* GETTING OUT?

1. Do you spend a disproportionate amount of time before every date trying to think up creative excuses for canceling? YES ___ No ___

2. Have you ever thought that it would be ridiculous to wash your hair for a date, since, after all, you washed it a mere four days ago?
YES ___ No ___

3. Has he ever proudly announced, "Mother is my best friend—I tell her *everything*"? YES ___ No ___

4. When you're out with him, do you feel under no obligation to make your usual, halfhearted, "Oh, let *me* get this one" lunge for the check?
YES ___ No ___

5. Do you—the same woman who has spent many pleasant hours poring over bridal magazines and fantasizing about your own nuptials— find yourself thinking, "I can't believe he's getting so serious so quickly"?
YES ___ No ___

6. When he asks if he can come in after a date, do you leap out of the car, saying, "That would really be a problem for my cats—they have terrible allergies"?
YES ___ No ___

7. If a friend spots the two of you together, do you phone her the instant you get home to let her know you're not really *dating,* per se?
YES ___ No ___

8. Do you make it a regular practice to bring others— relatives, friends, passing vagrants—along to your romantic rendezvous, declaring, "The more the merrier"?
YES ___ No ___

9. Do you urge him not to call, saying, "I'm really not a phone person"?
YES ___ No ___

10. Have you, after fooling around with him, announced, "I'm a very private person, and I would feel violated if you told anyone you'd touched me—or even spoken to me"?
YES ___ No ___

■ *If you answered yes to more than two of these*
questions, a ditch is in your immediate future.

TROLLING

Trolling is characterized by excessive eyelash-batting, shameless flirting, and wild sex—with any man *except* your boyfriend. "I was always trying to pretend to other guys that I was unattached," says Erin. "Whenever I went to a party, I'd spend hours trying to make myself look good for the single guys who would be there. By the end, I was putting way more effort into my two-minute encounters with the cute waiter at the coffee shop than into my live-in relationship."

DROWNING IN
YOUR OWN ANALYSIS

Your relationship consists primarily of talking about the problems in your relationship—even if you've only been going out for three weeks. "It got so that we weren't living the relationship, just dissecting it twenty-four hours a day," says Anita. "We'd try to stop, but it was impossible. The problems were so glaring."

MAKING EXCUSES FOR HIM

You tell yourself that it's of no import that he doesn't call when he said he would—he's under a lot of pressure at work. You turn a blind eye to his habit of ogling other women when he's out with you—it just means that he appreciates the female form. And so what if he never tells you he loves you? He's a guy's guy, that's all.[1] "Dean was planning to have Thanksgiving dinner with some of his friends, and I thought of course he'd get around to inviting me," says Marta. "He never did, and I was crushed. But I managed to convince myself that what he'd done wasn't so bad. After all, he'd only been sleeping with me for a few months —he'd known *them* for years."

LOSING THAT LOVING FEELING

When he reaches for your hand while walking down the street, you snatch it away and say, "It's too hot to hold hands." When he gazes soulfully into your eyes, you snap, "That's really not your most attractive facial expression." And his pet name for you, the one that used to make you feel all warm inside, now sends you into a blind rage. "When my boyfriend first started call-

---

[1] If he's treating you so cavalierly, chances are good that he's thinking about dumping *you*. Fortunately, there is something you can do: dump him first. This is known in the industry as a *preemptive strike*. In essence, you quit before you're fired—a bold maneuver we heartily recommend, since it enables you to exit the relationship with a shred of dignity. If you're going to lose him anyway, you might as well pretend it was your decision. In our experience, the only thing worse than ditching is *being* ditched.

ing me 'Minky,' I thought it was kind of goofy but very sweet," remembers Nora. "I knew the prognosis for the relationship wasn't good the day I told him that if he ever called me that again, I'd strangle him."

SHIRKING

You can't be bothered to meet the minimum licensing requirements for girlfriends: initiating the odd phone call, displaying concern should he fall ill, knowing and/or caring where he is on a Saturday night. "When I first started seeing Lawrence, I bought him little presents all the time," remembers Elyse. "But the last year we were together, I just wasn't motivated to get him anything, not even a birthday card. At the last minute, I rummaged around the office and found a card that said, 'Happy birthday from all of us,' crossed out the 'all of us' and scribbled in 'me.'"

BOXING YOURSELF
INTO A CORNER

You believe there's only one way to quash your doubts about the relationship: become even more seriously involved with the guy. Your thinking goes something like this: *If we move in together,*

[QUIZ TWO]

You're in a serious relationship, and you're wondering

AM I HAPPY—*or* HOMICIDAL?

1. When he tells you he has a cold, is your first response not "I'll be right over with some chicken soup," but "Well, you'd better not have given it to me"?
YES ___ NO ___

2. Do even his best qualities annoy you? (e.g., "Yes, he's brilliant and a witty conversationalist, but *must* we have meaningful, provocative discussions morning, noon, and night?")
YES ___ NO ___

3. Have you stopped reading his horoscope?
YES ___ NO ___

4. Do you tell yourself, "Well, who cares if we never have sex anymore? Married couples almost never have sex"?
YES ___ NO ___

5. At dinner, are you too distracted to make conversation because you're looking around the restaurant at all the couples who seem happier than you are?
YES ___ NO ___

6. Do you find yourself weeping in the bathtub on a regular basis?
YES ___ NO ___

7. Have you ever wondered whether he's having an affair, then thought, "Well if he is, I wish the two of them the very best"?
YES ___ NO ___

8. When you're kissing him, do you fantasize that you're with another man—or alone?
YES ___ NO ___

9. Do you feel like a trapped animal every time someone asks, "When are you two going to tie the knot already?"
YES ___ NO ___

10. Do you have a tendency to treat him like a flunkie? (e.g., "Get me a drink, pronto.")
YES ___ NO ___

■ *If you answered yes to more than two of these questions, there's no time to waste. Call in sick to work and devote the rest of the day to finishing this book.*

or get married, I'll settle down and stop feeling so rest-less and dissatisfied all the time. "My relationship with Phil was pretty much a disaster from Day One, and I spent most of my time and energy wondering whether we should stay together," says Janine. "After five years, things were worse than ever, but I decided we should get married. I figured if I took some decisive action, I'd stop vacillating and we could be happy. Wrong. The marriage lasted less than a year."

GENERAL MALAISE

You have all the symptoms of depression—listlessness, lack of enthusiasm about the future, general feelings of unhappiness and despair—but every mental-health professional you consult refuses to prescribe Prozac and urges you instead to dump your boyfriend.

Did you experience a thrill of recognition while reading the above list? If so, it's possible that you have a very low irritation threshold. But it's far more likely that you're about to embark on an important rite of passage in a woman's life: dumping a guy.

CHAPTER TWO

Getting in Touch with Your Inner Coward

Fear of ditching is not just a female phenomenon. Men, too, suffer this affliction. Like women, men don't relish saying, "I never want to see you again." Instead, they try to communicate the message indirectly. Just ask any woman who's sat by the phone, refusing to abandon her post for anything except the most dire medical emergency, waiting in vain to hear from a guy who told her, as he slunk off into the night, "I'll call you sometime."

Yet, although men can be quite cowardly, fear of ditching is one realm in which women reign supreme. But there's no need to castigate *ourselves* too harshly for this failing—really, society as a whole is to blame.

Consider the different messages men and women receive. Women are told that it's better to be with a man, any man, than to be alone; men are told that while a relationship does have a few benefits, like ensuring a steady supply of sex, it entails a significant loss of freedom. Women are told that the chances of finding a man who wants to settle down are roughly the same as the chances of finding the perfect little black dress, heavily discounted, an hour before a party; men are told that the chances of finding a woman who wants to settle down are the same as the chances of drawing another breath. Naturally, then, women find the prospect of ending a relationship quite a bit more frightening than men do.

This is particularly true if the romance has been serious, in which case your identity has become connected to the dumpee's. Everyone else treats you as one half of a pair, and you're used to thinking of yourself that way, too. You have your little rituals, in-jokes, and a shared history. Moreover, the dumpee knows you and cares for you in a way no one else does. Breaking up, then, will entail real loss and pain. So instead of telling him the relationship is over, you waver. "Maybe I'm just taking him for granted." Or "Maybe this is my last chance to get married and have children." Or "I've already invested so much time in this relationship . . ."

Even if you've only gone out with the guy a few times, you're probably wringing your hands and

BREAKUP MYTHS

MEN DUMP, WOMEN GET DUMPED

Clearly, a notion propagated by a bitter male dumpee with a wild imagination.

ANY RELATIONSHIP CAN BE FIXED, IF YOU'RE PREPARED TO WORK HARD ENOUGH

This might be true, but it would be rather distressing to learn that it *isn't* after several decades in a bad relationship, when the only man who has any interest in your body is your geriatrician.

BEING SINGLE IS A NIGHTMARE

We won't lie to you: it's no picnic. But it is considerably better than being in a relationship that makes you unhappy.

IT'S IMPOSSIBLE TO MEET NICE SINGLE MEN

No, there are plenty of nice single men out there, and it gets much easier to meet them when *you're* actually single. Remember: you can't meet Mr. Right until you dump Mr. Wrong.

asking yourself, "What if he *is* the man for me, and I haven't given him a fair chance?" In this case, however, what really scares you is the *process* of ditching. You can't think of a way to disguise the fact that you're just not attracted to the dumpee; you simply don't know him well enough yet to claim that you're ditching him for anything aside from his lack of charisma or sex appeal. And you're concerned that he'll think it's a little presumptuous of you to break up with him when you've only known for him for forty-eight hours, and might say something like, "What do you mean 'break up'? I didn't realize we were going out."

Whatever the length of the relationship you're contemplating ending, chances are good that you're scared witless and you're at a total loss as to how to go about it. Rejecting him outright just seems too brutal—for both of you. He might get upset and say or do something that hurts your feelings. Or he might try to persuade you to reconsider—Lord knows, when *you've* been dumped, your first reaction has always been to beg for mercy. You're afraid that if you encountered even the tiniest bit of resistance, you'd cave and tell the dumpee, "You're quite right, sweetie. Let's keep seeing each other."

So instead of proceeding with the ditch, you put it off. Just until you're feeling a bit stronger.

A truly determined coward can squander months or even years before she gets around to dumping a guy, and then she wastes even more time berating herself for the amount of time she wasted in the first place. There's only one way to avoid this sad fate: think through every aspect of the ditch, so you know what to expect at every stage. Once you understand the process fully, it won't seem quite so daunting. Read on.

CHAPTER THREE

Cling-ons and Other Difficult-to-Dump Men
A Typology

Every man has his own distinct personality, interests, and values, and it is important to recognize and respect his individuality. At least while you're going out with him. But when it comes time to give him the heave-ho, you must face facts: there are essentially only ten types of men.

T Y P E   O N E

THE CLING-ON

When you first meet a Cling-on, he seems like a dream come true: attentive, supremely confident, and—best of all—not afraid of commitment. Usually, the Cling-on is also extremely presentable, well-traveled, and possesses excellent social skills. When you describe him to your mother, she says, "Oh, I like the sound of *this* one"—your first clue that something is not quite right.

After just a few dates, you realize he's a little *too* attentive. He won't stop with the phone calls and unannounced visits. In fact, he's a smotherer: corny greeting cards, deliveries of roses—so many you feel like you're in a funeral home—and premature invitations to meet his parents are his stock-in-trade. It's not that he's needy, it's just that he believes you simply can't get enough of him.

The hallmark of a romance with a Cling-on is that the normal stages of a relationship are accelerated: you go from attraction to revulsion in a matter of weeks, if not days. One of the major difficulties in shedding such a man is that you've often said things to him in the initial stages of infatuation that are very difficult to unsay a mere forty-eight hours later—for example, "I think I may love you, too." The Cling-on is blessed with a prodigious memory for such remarks and will not let you forget them in a hurry.

To make matters worse, his reaction to polite signs of disengagement is one of serene disbelief. The Cling-on thinks that if he presses his suit just a little more forcefully, you will come to your senses.

The problem, he believes, is that you don't know him well enough. Yet.

FAVORITE EXPRESSION: *"Hey kiddo, what's with the long face?"*

FAVORITE POSSESSION: A collection of costly sweaters with very busy patterns

TYPE TWO

THE TIN MAN

The Tin Man is the Cling-on's polar opposite: distant, inscrutable, and taciturn. All of which makes him an intriguing challenge. You figure that, like his namesake in *The Wizard of Oz,* the Tin Man *must* have a heart somewhere beneath that cool exterior.

This notion is not *completely* absurd. The Tin Man does, after all, boast a romantic résumé that's both long and impressive, which suggests that intimacy is not repellent to him. He often reinforces this illusion by waxing poetic about another woman for whom he still carries a torch. You convince yourself this is a hopeful sign: if he feels so strongly about her, he can feel even more strongly about you. It's only a matter of time.

Which is why you hang in there, despite his dazzling displays of indifference. He rarely phones, and when he does, you feel such an immense rush of relief that you don't question his pathetic excuses: "I was in Fort Lauderdale and didn't have a calling card," or, "Has it really been two weeks? I've been so busy at work, guess I lost track of time."

In Stage One of a relationship with a Tin Man, you excuse his coolness as evidence of an unhappy childhood: *He's psychologically scarred because his parents never expressed their love for him—I can heal him.* In Stage Two, after you've met his remarkably warm and well-adjusted family, you begin thinking the problem is with you: you're not pretty enough, or sophisticated enough, or mysterious enough to keep his interest. By Stage Three, your entire existence revolves around trying to win his approval.

The longer the two of you are together, the less affectionate he is (if you protest this state of affairs, however, he will suggest that you're neurotic and something of a Cling-on in your own right). Which may be why the sex never ceases to be exciting, even though the Tin Man's technique is utterly devoid of emotion: it's just about the only indication you ever get that he wants to be with you.

On paper, the Tin Man looks like the easiest kind of man to ditch because you get so little from him. In reality, however, he's one of the most diffi-cult types to leave, and the reason is *you*. You don't want to go until you have indisputable proof that he cares about you. Just one tiny problem: you're never going to get it.

FAVORITE EXPRESSION: *"Whatever."*

FAVORITE POSSESSION: His car

T Y P E   T H R E E

THE UP-AND-COMER

The Up-and-Comer isn't hard to recognize: he's remarkably talented, self-disciplined, and am-bitious. Yet, he's no back-stabbing climber—even those who envy him grudgingly admit he's a gen-uinely nice person. You're thrilled to be going out with such a decent, kindhearted, upstanding guy.

Frankly, you're a little in awe of him. After all, the two of you have lived approximately the same num-ber of years on this earth, but anyone looking at your respective résumés would think he had a good fifty years on you. Of course, there's a reason for the dis-parity: while he was setting goals—and meeting them—you were sprawled on the couch watching *Seinfeld* reruns. No longer, you vow. Inspired by the Up-and-Comer, you're turning over a new leaf. You're going to apply yourself, for a change.

But after a few weekends in the office (the better part of which are spent snooping through co-workers' desks and raiding the candy machine), you're forced to confront the truth. You just don't have it in you to be an Up-and-Comer.

And let's face it: there's a whole world out there that you wouldn't be able to experience if your nose was constantly to the grindstone!

What rapidly becomes apparent, however, is that you'll be experiencing that world on your own ninety-five percent of the time, because the Up-and-Comer has a *very* busy schedule. When you're not with him, you feel neglected; when you are with him, you feel like a slug by comparison—and a defensive slug, at that. It really bothers you that his whole existence is so carefully mapped out, with no room for spontaneity—or you.

Still, you can't quite bring yourself to take action. Thus far, hanging on to his coattails has pretty much been your only accomplishment in life—you're not prepared to let go simply because you're lonely and resentful. Furthermore, you know that if you ditch him, not only will your friends and family think you've lost your mind, but you'll be hearing about his triumphs for the rest of your days—most likely on the national news.

FAVORITE EXPRESSION: *"You know, Pumpkin, if you spent a little less time gossiping with your friends, there's no telling what you could do!"*

FAVORITE POSSESSION: His meticulously organized Filofax

TYPE FOUR

THE HARMLESS WEIRDO

At first, you think the Harmless Weirdo is adorably eccentric, offbeat, and intelligent— an iconoclast, really. Yes, he has a few unusual quirks and mannerisms, but he's no boring, cookie-cutter frat boy. In short, he's totally unlike any other man you've ever dated, which strikes you as a good thing.

Your view changes, radically, the evening you proudly introduce him to your friends. In front of everyone you know, your new suitor relates an anecdote about a bus trip he once took that goes on forever and has no apparent point. Then, when the conversation turns to politics, he hijacks it, launching into a long, unstoppable tirade about the unacknowledged link between diet soda and brain damage. In a moment of sickening clarity, you become aware that you are dating a deeply odd individual. He's the nerd from chemistry class, traveling incognito thanks to a pair of chinos from The Gap.

Moments after this realization, you put dumping him at the very top of your to-do list. But the Harmless Weirdo isn't exactly attuned to social cues and fundamentally doesn't understand that he's being ditched. Long after you've shown him the door, he'll still call and drop by with no warning, as though nothing has changed. Although he's not physically threatening, psychologically, he's a menace. He's a reminder that at times, your judgment can be very poor indeed.

FAVORITE EXPRESSION: *"Without these glasses, I'm legally blind."*

FAVORITE POSSESSION: His iguana

T Y P E   F I V E

THE REJECT ADDICT

When you first meet the Reject Addict, you have no idea who you're dealing with. You simply think he's a charismatic, profoundly sexy man who's intensely interested in every facet of your being. What a shame that you're already in a relationship. But that doesn't deter the Reject Addict. In fact, he pursues you assiduously: bantering phone calls, playful E-mails, impromptu invitations to go for coffee. Flattered, you think, "Well, there's no harm in just being friends."

In no time at all, you're convinced that he's your soul mate. For one thing, he doesn't find it the slightest bit boring when you talk about the problems you're having with your boyfriend. He helps you see that, contrary to what you may have thought, you're mired in a miserable romance. He tells you he knows exactly how you feel: he hasn't had much luck with relationships either. Curiously enough, he's hounded by women who aren't suitable for him; the ones who would be perfect are always unavailable. Before long, your platonic get-togethers have undergone a slight transformation: they now include furtive embraces . . . at a minimum.

Sex with the Reject Addict, even if it never goes beyond a few stolen kisses, is mind-blowing. It's illicit, intense, and freighted with tragedy: you're star-crossed lovers, and the pain is deliciously unbearable.

Then it dawns on you: you don't have to suffer like this! You promptly ditch your boyfriend and call the Reject Addict to tell him the good news. There's a long pause, after which he mumbles, "Uh, I'm kind of busy. Let me call you back."

But he doesn't, not that day or the next. Nor

does he respond to any of your frantic, rambling messages. You alternate between weeping in your darkened bedroom and psychoanalyzing him with your friends, all of whom agree that he must have been scared off by the strength of his own feelings.

A few months later, just when you're starting to date again, the Reject Addict resurfaces, begging forgiveness. You're thrilled to see him, but sternly announce, "Regaining my trust is going to take a *very* long time." And it does. Six whole days, in fact. But wait, where's he gone?

The Reject Addict is one of the most dangerous men you'll ever meet. He's intoxicatingly charming, and so persuasive that he actually seems sincere when he says, for the eleventh time, "I've changed. This time I'm *sure* you're what I want." Once you're on to him and refuse to fall for his lines yet again, he loves you more than ever; rejection only inflames his passion, which is why he's so difficult to ditch. You have to do it over and over and—well, you get the idea.

Remember: the Reject Addict *never* changes. He loves the chase, but always throws back the catch.

FAVORITE EXPRESSION: *"Where have you been all my life?"*

FAVORITE POSSESSION: His answering machine

OL' MONEYBAGS

Although Ol' Moneybags can be any age, he tends to be a little long in the tooth, since great wealth is rarely acquired overnight. He's not exactly easy on the eyes, but he does have a few sterling qualities: he takes you to the finest restaurants, showers you with shiny baubles, and is able to get front-row theater tickets on a moment's notice. Every date with him is like a new episode of *Lifestyles of the Rich and Famous*. Your parents are as happy as you've ever seen them in your adult life.

After a while, however, you begin having heretical thoughts: "What good is a $300 dinner if I'm not in love with the man?" When he sees that you're getting restless, Ol' Moneybags ponies up ever more lavish trinkets. But it's no use. Even a diamond-encrusted watch can't fill the void in your heart.

Yet part of you is reluctant to give him the kiss-off. You've grown accustomed to a lifestyle that you have no hope of replicating on your own. To make matters worse, all your friends are encouraging you to work on the relationship—at least until they've had a chance to spend a weekend at Ol'

Moneybags' country estate.

FAVORITE EXPRESSION: *"Put that on my account."*

FAVORITE POSSESSION: You

T Y P E   S E V E N

THE LAPDOG

The Lapdog is truly one of the kindest and most helpful men you will ever meet. Eager to please, he is unfailingly loyal, obedient, and delighted by any scrap of affection you toss his way. He drops everything when you have a crisis, and has no qualms whatsoever about dashing out to the store when your stock of feminine hygiene products is running low. You're ecstatic: this is exactly the kind of man you've been looking for. And for a while, everything is great.

Well, not *everything*. The truth is, he shows far too little interest in hot, steamy sex. He's much too respectful, for instance, to rip off your clothes. And every time you close your eyes and try to fantasize that he's ravishing you, he breaks your concentration by saying something like "Am I doing this right? Do you want me to slow down?" Or worse yet, "How can I pleasure you?" By the end of this pop quiz, you feel like investing in a good vibrator.

As time goes on, other things start to bother you, too. Like the way that he defers to your wishes all the time. You always thought you wanted to be worshiped, but in reality, it brings out the worst in you. Since you're certain he wouldn't dream of looking at another woman, you feel free to carp, criticize, and neglect him shamelessly. You find yourself testing him—"forgetting" to invite him to a party, bossing him around mercilessly—in the hope that he'll stand up to you. If he did, you're convinced that you'd revert to your usual affable self and the two of you would live happily ever after. But the Lapdog is too good-natured to bite back.

He is perhaps *the* most difficult type to dump, because you know you really should appreciate such a wonderful guy, and besides, you depend on him for every little thing. Even when you derive no pleasure from his companionship, you're loath to send the Lapdog to the pound. But the truth is, it would be the kindest thing to do: he would be adopted immediately.

FAVORITE EXPRESSION: *"You're the boss."*

FAVORITE POSSESSION: Bottle of Woolite, because you insist that he do your fine washables by hand

THE SEXUAL SAVANT

Like his first cousin, the idiot savant, the Sexual Savant exhibits genius in just one highly specialized area. From the start, you're aware that he's not exactly a towering intellect, but you don't care. So prodigious are his erotic gifts that initially, they seem to compensate (and then some) for his deficits in other areas. For the first few months, your relationship with the Sexual Savant is conducted almost exclusively in the nude, at your behest. You are blissfully happy.

Then, one Sunday morning, you decide to try something novel: a conversation. After ten minutes, however, it becomes very clear that the two of you have next to nothing in common. Your reaction: haul him back to the bedroom, where you are able to forget—for quite a remarkable length of time—that you ever had this revelation.

Unfortunately, this state of denial cannot be maintained forever. Eventually, the day arrives when you yearn for a multidimensional—or at least two-dimensional—relationship, and although it's heart-wrenching to contemplate giving up the perquisites of your current situation, you resolve to do just that. After a few more carnal interludes, that is.

FAVORITE EXPRESSION: *"Give me a few minutes, and I could do it again."*

FAVORITE POSSESSION: Massage oil

TYPE NINE

THE MEMORIALIST

The Memorialist is a creative type—a writer, painter, actor, musician, filmmaker, etc.—which at first makes him seem incredibly sensitive and deep. You love listening to him talk about his struggle to produce Art in a culture that views True Artists as commodities. You adore going to parties with him and passing yourself off as a Muse, of sorts. You relish accompanying him to the smoky, poorly-lit bars that he and his friends frequent, even though you usually have to pick up the tab.

After a while, however, you start to wonder why it is, exactly, that the Memorialist spends so much more time talking about art than creating it. It occurs to you that maybe his lifestyle is a little *too* alternative: he doesn't have a regular paycheck, normal work hours, or even one decent-looking suit. And what you first thought was an artistic temperament now strikes you as raging egomania. The man simply won't stop talking about himself. Coddling this brooding, tortured artiste is draining the lifeblood right out of you.

You know it's high time to give him the boot, but you're reluctant to do so. He's bound to stage a few melodramatic, grandiose fits. Worse yet, he might memorialize you—the last woman who dumped him was the inspiration for a work of art entitled "Fat Girl Walking." Years after dumping the Memorialist, you still quake with fear that any day now he'll produce a thinly veiled, deeply unflattering record of your relationship, which will become an instant classic.

FAVORITE EXPRESSION: *"The masses are asses."*

FAVORITE POSSESSION: His agent's home phone number

THE GARDEN-VARIETY MAN

As his name suggests, the Garden-Variety Man is the most numerous in kind. He cannot be reduced to a caricature, because his behavior falls within the normal range: he's reasonably mature, perfectly nice, and displays no overt signs of pathology. Frequently, he's not just your boy-friend—he's your best friend.

You really care for him, but the relationship simply isn't working anymore. Maybe you love him, but you're just not *in love* with him. Maybe you want to get married, but he just isn't ready. Maybe you've started fooling around with someone else, and he has very strict views about monogamy.

Whatever the reason, breaking up with him is going to be very painful for both of you. There is only one consolation—at least he's not a Cling-on.

———

Did you recognize your soon-to-be dumpee in the typology?[1] Good! Knowing him for who he really is will help you make the difficult decisions that lie ahead. But enough about him—let's talk about you.

---

[1]If not, it's possible that he is a hybrid of two types: an Ol' Moneybags with a touch of the Cling-on, for example.

CHAPTER FOUR

The Kinder, Gentler Ditch

Y ou probably think of yourself as the type of woman who would never hurt a dumpee any more than she absolutely had to. Well, it's time for some ruthless self-examination. You need to analyze the ditching methods you've used in the past and honestly assess the devastation you've wreaked on your dumpees.

GOING AWOL

T he woman simply stops returning her suitor's calls, hoping that he'll get the hint and she'll get rid of him without ever having to say a word. This entails several weeks of religiously screening her calls and skulking around town. If he somehow manages to reach her by phone, she lies: "I'm on the other line, I'll call you back."

He doesn't get the hint and keeps calling—or he's insulted to be treated like a creep who must be avoided at all costs.

The carpe diem ditch

The woman wants out, but refuses to leave until she can blame the breakup on the dumpee. So she waits until he does one tiny thing wrong, then seizes the day: she blows his misstep wildly out of proportion and presents it as the sole cause of the ditch. "I'd wanted to dump Bill for a while, but I felt embarrassed because my reasons seemed so shallow. For instance, I couldn't stand his clothes," says Susan. "So I lay in wait for him to make a mistake, and finally he did: he didn't plan anything for my birthday. I ran with that. I exploded and told him I couldn't possibly be with a man who didn't organize a party or at least a dinner."

The dumpee knows that he's being unfairly blamed for the ditch, and the sense of injustice rankles.

The human repellent

A most unusual strategy. The woman tries to drive the dumpee away by making herself as unappealing as possible—peppering her speech with profanities, drinking vast quantities of beer, and/or slouching around in ratty sweatpants.

Far from being repulsed, the dumpee is even more attracted: she's one of the guys, only better-looking.

ADVERTISING FOR YOUR OWN REPLACEMENT

Rarely used beyond the second-date stage. The ditcher tries to fob the dumpee off on another woman, figuring that he won't be upset about being ditched if a new romantic interest is waiting in the wings. This method requires superb salesmanship. The dumpee must be marketed to the new woman in a way that doesn't arouse her suspicion: "If he's so great, why don't *you* want him?"

The dumpee is offended by the presumption that he can't get dates on his own.

HIRING A HIT MAN

Distinctive for its immaturity. After many hilarious prep sessions, the woman deputizes a friend to tell the dumpee, "You know, I don't think she's over her last boyfriend," or, "I think she's afraid of intimacy, she always runs in the other direction whenever she meets a great guy," etc. The ditcher moves in for the kill only after the friend has stabbed the dumpee in the heart a few times.

The dumpee is outraged when he figures out he's been set up — and humiliated, because he believes, quite rightly, that everyone in town is laughing at him.

THE COLD FISH

The woman stops having sex with the dumpee, hoping that he'll be so frustrated he'll welcome a ditch. If he tries to touch her, she either flinches and pulls away, or says, "Oh please, not now." Whenever he asks her what's wrong, she stares off into the distance, sighs, and finally says, "I don't know. I just don't feel like having sex. Ever."

After trying every aphrodisiac on the market, the dumpee decides he's dating a traditional woman who's deeply uncomfortable with premarital sex, and proposes marriage.

THE PASSIVE-AGGRESSIVE DITCH

The woman tries to get out of doing the dirty work by making the dumpee so angry that *he* will break up with *her*. "I did things like telling him to meet me somewhere at 3:00 and not showing up till 5:00," says Joan. "But instead of getting furious, he went to even greater lengths to please me, like making me special dinners."

Ineffective: the dumpee thinks she's bitchy and demanding—a turn-on for some men.

THE INSTALLMENT PLAN

The woman dumps a guy in stages, for three reasons: she believes it's more humane to give him time to get used to the idea, she wants to keep him hanging on in case she changes her mind at some point mid-ditch, and she hopes that by easing out of the relationship gradually, the decision will seem less like hers alone and more like it's mutual. "First I told him that I wasn't very happy in the relationship. Then about a month later, I suggested some time apart," says Franny. "Next I said I thought we ought to see other people. Finally, after four months, I told him I thought we should end things."

Barbaric, because it prolongs the dumpee's agony and gives him false hope.

━━━━━

There are two problems with all these methods: they're highly inefficient, and they make the dumpee suffer more than is absolutely necessary. So what is the kinder, gentler way to dump a guy? The clean break: you tell him in a relatively direct, timely, and non-negotiable fashion that the relationship is at an end, and you allow him to move

Ten Priceless Pearls
of Ditching Wisdom

Before embarking on the adventure that is ditching, spare a moment to pay homage to all the women who have gone before you. They were the true pioneers, and it is to them that we owe thanks for the following pearls of wisdom.

1. No reason for leaving should ever be dismissed as too shallow.

Don't stay in a relationship simply because you feel you lack sufficient justification to end it. Remember: you don't have to have a good reason to leave—you only need *to tell others* you had one.

2. Don't be afraid to leave before you've lined up a replacement.

If you feel you can't dump a guy until another one is waiting in the wings, you might wind up postponing the ditch for months or even years. Besides, jumping from relationship to relationship can be quite messy, because there's usually some overlap.

3. Don't broadcast your plans.

The dumpee should not be the last person on the planet to find out he's being ditched. If you need a sounding board, talk to one or two incredibly discreet friends; to be on the safe side, we advise choosing a confidante who resides overseas.

4. Do it yourself.

Don't try to force *him* to break up with *you*—it's cowardly and manipulative, if not downright cruel. Besides, no one should be under the impression that *he* dumped *you,* lest your social standing be adversely affected.

5. DON'T PROLONG THE AGONY.

Dumping a guy is not unlike waxing your legs: in both cases, you're getting rid of something unwanted and it hurts like hell, but if it's done in slow motion, it's a form of torture.

6. DON'T WING IT.

A good breakup doesn't just happen. It is planned with the same attention to detail as any other life-altering ceremony. How, when, where, what to say, and, of course, what to wear—all should be considered very carefully.

7. HONESTY IS NOT *ALWAYS* THE BEST POLICY.

The dumpee doesn't need to know, for example, that you're having an affair. There is a time and a place for such confessions: your therapist's office. Such information would only hurt the dumpee gratuitously. The explanation you give him should have the whiff of honesty, but not the stench of truth.

8. DON'T LEAVE THE DOOR AJAR.

If you're certain you want to be rid of him for all time, it's unfair to give the dumpee false hope. Even if you think there's a possibility that in the future you might change your mind, it's best not to tell him so now. He'd be more inclined to get back together if you didn't subject him to an ugly, on-again, off-again breakup.

9. NEVER LOSE SIGHT OF THE PR ASPECTS.

When you initiate a rupture, your every action —before, during, and after the breakup—can become grist for the gossip mill, particularly if the dumpee is heartbroken or out for vengeance. Even before you dump him, then, you must start thinking like a spin doctor: how can I play this in a way that won't harm, and might actually enhance, my reputation?

10. REMEMBER: FOR EVERY MILE OF ROAD, THERE ARE TWO MILES OF DITCH.

on with a minimum of fuss.

You might think, "That sounds kinder to *him,* but what about me?" Well, it's true that you're deprived of the opportunity to play some of your favorite head games, but the sacrifice is worth it. You get the result you want in less time, with less risk of permanently alienating the dumpee.

There's just one drawback to this method: it's the most frightening one for a coward. Which is why the rest of this book is devoted to helping you master your fears so that you, too, can execute a kinder, gentler ditch.

CHAPTER FIVE

The Ditching Hour

Scheduling Your Breakup

Perhaps it seems to you that there's no such thing as a good time to dump a guy—and that all days and hours are equally inopportune.

Not true! Some times *are* considerably better than others. For instance, it's unspeakably rude to drop the bombshell while he's still at the office and isn't at liberty to fall apart (and imprudent to do so while *you're* still at work, since the dumpee might run over and cause a scene). On the other hand, breaking the news too late in the evening would be unwise, unless you relish fielding weepy phone calls throughout the night.

The ideal time for a ditch is Friday, between 7:00 and 8:00 P.M. He has the whole weekend to lick his wounds, and if you wrap things up quickly, you may be able to squeeze in another date that very evening.[1]

Now that we've ascertained the most auspicious ditching hour, there's some bad news: no more than two weeks should elapse between the day you decide to dump a guy and the day you actually do it. We understand that arranging your breakup can take some time, particularly if you're terminating a serious relationship, and we would never advise rushing into it without careful planning. Nevertheless, any more than two weeks and you're not planning—you're procrastinating.

You may protest: I can't possibly ditch him in that time frame, it's just not convenient for me! Let's examine your reasons, to see if they're at all legitimate.

WE'RE ABOUT TO GO AWAY TOGETHER

Sharing a hotel room with a guy you're planning to dump would be a nightmare. He'd have sex-

---

[1]If you and your dumpee are in different time zones, it may be impossible to coordinate a 7:00 P.M. Friday breakup. If, for instance, he's in London and you're in Los Angeles, you would have to call him at 11:00 A.M. your time to catch him at 7:00 P.M. his time, thus giving him a minimum of six hours to pester you at work. If you face such a scheduling dilemma, dump him at the first opportunity on Saturday.

ual expectations, and you'd have two courses of action: meet them, or pretend to have a yeast infection for fourteen days straight.

Sadly, you must dump him and forego the vacation. If, post-ditch, he suggests that you still go away together "just as friends," don't fall for it. Once you got to your destination, he'd almost certainly say, "What's your problem? Friends have sex all the time!"

You may be thinking, "But my ticket isn't refundable—I'm going to lose a lot of money!" To which we reply, it's a small price to pay for such an invaluable lesson: you should always purchase travel insurance, and cultivate friendships with unethical doctors who will gladly vouch that you're too ill to travel.

IT'S THE HOLIDAY SEASON

At first blush, December seems the cruelest month for a breakup. But actually, the festive season lends itself quite nicely to ditching. The dumpee already has plans to see friends and family, so his support system will be in place. Plus, he'll have some time off work to mope—and plenty of invitations to parties attended by single women in shimmery little dresses, who will take his mind off his troubles.

My birthday is coming up, and he's already planned a big party

A legitimate excuse. If you ditch him before the soirée, he will cancel it (a hideous social faux pas for which you will be blamed) or, worse yet, pull a martyr routine and bravely insist on holding it anyway (a maddening attention-getting stunt that will almost certainly deflect attention from the guest of honor). You can't ditch him too soon afterward, either—seven full days must elapse. Any fewer and you risk a public relations disaster: all the partygoers who call to thank him will be informed that you expressed your gratitude by dumping him.

He's already booked a ticket to come visit me

The only thing worse than being dumped on one's own turf is being dumped in foreign territory with no option but to rely on one's ditcher for room and board. It's not so pleasant for the ditcher, either, who's stuck playing hostess to a brooding, resentful, and possibly highly ornery houseguest.

Which is why, if you're in a long-distance relationship, you should do the polite thing: ditch him by phone, even if he's on the way out the door to the airport. He may kick up a fuss and say, "I'm coming anyway—we need to talk about this in person." If he cannot be dissuaded, tell him that you'll meet him for an hour or so to talk things over, but forewarn him: seeing him is not going to change your mind—and he'll need to arrange his own accommodations.

A word about finances. If you begged him to come visit, you must offer to reimburse him for the plane ticket. If, however, the rendezvous was his big idea, or even a mutual decision, you are under no obligation. Think of it this way: he'll be saving a bundle on his phone bills in the coming months.

Valentine's Day is coming up

In case you hadn't noticed, the average man couldn't care less about this particular holiday, so don't worry about offending *him*. If you, however, feel you can't live without shipments of roses, mushy cards, and fancy dinners on February 14, don't wait two weeks to dump him: do it this very minute. You need to get cracking if you want to line up a new benefactor in time for Valentine's Day.

He's in the midst of a terrible crisis

If he's studying for a critically important test, or preparing for a work project that will determine his future, or a member of his immediate family is deathly ill, this is the time to show some compassion. Four weeks' worth, to be exact, during which period you should bide your time and feign interest.[2] It's the kind thing to do, but also the sensible thing: no one thinks highly of a woman who ditches a man three days before his Bar exam. Yes, it's a bit deceitful, but it won't require too much acting ability on your part, since he'll be distracted and won't have much time to spend with you, anyway.

I'm in the midst of a terrible crisis

Our condolences. But you shouldn't lean on a man, demanding support, favors, and limitless understanding, when you're planning to dump him as soon as the crisis is over. You're a strong, independent woman who can get through anything on her own! Besides, you should be using

---

[2]If his crisis won't be over in a month, however, it might be better for both of you if you bailed immediately. The longer you stick around, the more dependent he'll become and the more difficult it will be for you to leave.

your temporary vulnerability in more forward-looking ways—namely, to attract new men. Remember, men are suckers for needy women, so milk your crisis for all it's worth.

━━━━━━

Clearly, the vast majority of you have no excuse whatsoever for further procrastination. The clock is already ticking. You have two weeks, maximum, and there is much to be done.

CHAPTER SIX

Countdown to D-Day

In the days before the breakup, you may be tempted to wallow in self-pity, or while away the hours droning on to your friends about the difficult road that lies ahead. But this is no time for melodrama. It's the time to take action: your quality of life post-ditch may be negatively affected unless you attend to the following tasks.

GETTING YOUR STUFF BACK

You might be under the impression that, post-ditch, your dumpee will voluntarily return any personal property you have left at his home. Think again. "After I broke up with Mitchell, I realized I'd left my diaphragm at his apartment," says Yolanda. "He didn't give it back and there was no way to ask for it that wouldn't make him crazy with jealousy."[1]

---

[1] A reliable male source tells us that an ex's underwear is "the ultimate prize. It's like a medal. I would not return any underwear—I'd frame it." This man, by the way, is not a cross-dresser or a pervert with a panty fetish, but a Garden-Variety dumpee. Forewarned is forearmed.

As soon as you've scheduled your ditch, you must immediately begin repossessing your belongings. The preferred technique is to smuggle them out of his home a few items at a time. Resist the temptation to loot the place in a single evening. Running around in a frenzy, cramming your personal effects into a huge duffel bag, might arouse suspicion.

Some items may be too unwieldy to spirit away, in which case you will have no choice but to beg the dumpee to give them back post-ditch. But do so only if they are irreplaceable; niggardliness is a most unattractive quality in a ditcher. Just ask Marina, who was dumped by a man who thereafter badgered her with phone calls demanding the return of his toilet plunger. "I was floored. He could have bought a new one for $7 at any hardware store," she says. "After the third call, I went over to his house and left it on his doorstep with a huge red bow and a note that said, 'Here's your goddamned plunger.'" She now regrets that she refrained from adding a scatological reference or two.

Pre-ditch is also when you should begin returning his possessions. Again, do this in dribs and drabs, and as casually as possible: "Oh, here's

that book you loaned me. I finished it last night."
If you fail to heed this advice, be prepared: post-
ditch, he will have an excuse to bang on your door
at one in the morning, demanding the return of his
favorite baseball cap.

The preemptive muzzle

It's likely that your dumpee knows a few things
about you that you would never want publi-
cized. For instance, your entire sexual history,
complete with lapses in judgment and experimen-
tal phases; damning remarks you've made about
your friends; embarrassing medical problems; the
exam you failed or job you didn't get, the one no
one else even knows you were going for; and
assorted neurotic habits and mannerisms.
Understandably, you're concerned about the damage he could do to your reputation—*very* concerned if the dumpee is a Memorialist, or even just
a Garden-Variety raconteur.

You have only one course of action: you must
prevent him from even *thinking* about airing your
dirty laundry. Remember, you have quite a dossier
on him, too, and you must not let him forget it.
Out of the blue one evening, bring up a few
humiliating episodes from his past, then say, in a

ruminative tone, "It's funny, most people really don't know you very well. They would be so shocked if they ever heard some of this stuff."

The theory here is *mutual assured destruction* (MAD): you deter a potential enemy from going nuclear by letting him know that you have the capability to retaliate in kind. The result is that neither party is tempted to launch an attack, since both would be destroyed. MAD worked during the Cold War, and it can work for you, too.[2]

CALLING IN HIS IOU'S

Does he owe you any money? If you're not prepared to write off your losses, you must begin your crusade for repayment as soon as you schedule your ditch date. This can be tricky, because you don't want to tip him off as to why getting your $10 back is suddenly of such pressing importance. Here's a tried-and-true method: "Hon, I saw the greatest gift for you today, but I'm a little short on cash—any way you could pay me back now?"

---

[2]You may be thinking, "But my dumpee's a nice guy—he'd never do anything to hurt me." That may well be true, but you can't afford to take chances. Grief, stress, and jealousy can bring out a side of your dumpee that you've never seen before.

CALLING OFF YOUR IOU'S

Perhaps you owe him some trifling amount. If you have the means, pay him back immediately. It is the right and proper thing to do.

Not everyone, however, has the luxury of being proper. If you find yourself in straitened circumstances—for example, repaying him would require forgoing certain necessities (such as your personal trainer or weekly pedicure)—you should kick off your poor-little-me campaign well before you give him the heave-ho. The object is to present yourself as a damsel in such distress that only a mean-spirited tightwad would dream of demanding his money back. You might begin tonight, by asking, in your best this-is-just-a-hypothetical-question tone, "Do you think if a person declares bankruptcy, I would get—I mean, *she* would get—thrown in jail?"

CHANGING THE LOCKS

In the first flush of a romance, when it seems as though love will last forever, you frequently present your beau with certain tokens of intimacy: the keys to your home, the access code to your answering machine, your calling card number, and so on. Before the relationship screeches to a halt, you must take preventive measures to protect your privacy post-ditch.

This will not be as simple as asking for your keys back—the dumpee would be highly insulted to be treated like a common criminal. And besides, you'd never know if he's made copies or not.

At least a week before the breakup, request a new calling card and buy a new answering machine—or consider getting voice mail, because you can change your access code at the drop of a hat. And waste no time in making an appointment with a locksmith. A tip to the savvy shopper: you don't necessarily have to invest in a whole new lock—simply changing one of the cylinders in the existing lock often renders his key unusable, and saves you a tidy bundle.

PLANNING FOR LIFE WITHOUT A MANSERVANT

If there are chores you either can't or won't do on your own, such as hanging pictures or installing blinds, consider getting the prospective dumpee to lend a hand. The sooner you get him working for you, the better. Let's face it: it's hard to find good help these days.

Disposing of incriminating evidence

Think hard, very hard: does the dumpee have anything in his possession which, if revealed, would necessitate your immediate relocation to another country? Such as, say, those nude photos you allowed him to take one steamy evening, or the poem you wrote for him on your one-month anniversary, the one that rhymed "your hot throbbing member" with "the cold snows of December"?

If you have reason to believe that he has kept any particularly sordid souvenirs, ransack his apartment well before the ditch. If you are unable to locate the relics, you will have to broach the subject of their whereabouts, under the guise of wanting to view them again for erotic or sentimental purposes.

If he hauls out the offending items or you locate them on your own, wait until the last possible moment to filch them. If you do it too early, you risk detection. By the way, don't think of this as stealing. The only person who should have such incriminating items is your boyfriend, and this guy is about to be stripped of that title.

Harness the Power
of Your Own Mind

Visualizing your new life as a single woman

A thletes in pursuit of Olympic records commonly use positive visualization techniques to achieve their goals. The theory is simple: if you can imagine yourself succeeding at something, you can actually *make* it happen. Set aside an evening when you know you won't be disturbed, and discover the power of positive visualization.

The following exercises will require your full concentration, so it's important to establish the right atmosphere. Unplug the phone. Light a few candles. Put on some soft music, very low. Uncork a bottle of wine—red, preferably—and pour yourself a glass. Once you're relaxed, lie down on the ground and breathe deeply, focusing on the alignment of your spine: imagine that you are pressing each vertebra into the floor. You will know that you are doing this correctly when your mind is clear of all thoughts except one: it's time to invest in a softer carpet.

Now you are ready to begin visualizing your new life as a single woman! First, picture yourself on a sun-drenched beach, utterly alone. Yours are the only footprints in the sand. The dumpee is but a distant memory. Hear the sound of the waves crashing against the shore. Feel the warmth of the sea breeze, enveloping you like a whisper. Breathe the salt air, and know that you are free.

Next, picture yourself in a log cabin, stretched out in front of a roaring fire. Outside, all is still and snowy wonder. Looking at the majestic white-capped peaks, you feel at one with your surroundings. You can no longer conjure a clear image of the dumpee's face. Hear the crackle of the flames as they leap. Feel the heat, warming you through and through. Breathe deep the piney scent of wood smoke, and know that you are free.

Finally, picture this: You are lying on a satin sheet, eyes closed. Your well-toned body is arched with pleasure, responding to the gentle, patient caresses of a lean yet muscular, strong yet sensitive man who has no idea just how strikingly handsome he is. Dumpee? What dumpee? You have a vague recollection of dumping someone at some point, but no details are springing to mind. The man beside you is murmuring that he has never known a body as beautiful as yours, or a mind as fine, or a spirit as pure. Hear the certainty in his husky voice. Feel the tender promise of his touch. Breathe the pleasant musk of his freshly washed skin, and know that you are . . .

Drunk. Very drunk. Smashed, in fact, if you were able to convince yourself that the last scenario was actually taking place—or could *ever* take place. But there's no point in punishing yourself—live in the moment! Get off the floor, put on some decent music, crack open another bottle, and let the breakup celebration begin!

CHAPTER SEVEN

Mail-order Ditching

and Other Processes of Elimination

The time has come to consider the way in which you will break the sad news to the dumpee. The medium you select will set the tone for your breakup, so weigh your options carefully.

DEAR JOHN

Historically, the letter has been a favored medium: highbrow, civilized, and irrefutable. Today, it still has its advocates. "You can be clear, control the content, and there's no back talk," says Sarah, who selected this option to end a six-month relationship. "If you send him a letter, he can go back over it and read between the lines."

As with any challenging art form, she says, practice makes perfect. "The first paragraph should

remind him of your good qualities and wit. He
should initially be oblivious to the fact that it's a
'Dear John' letter," instructs Sarah. "But in the second paragraph, you lower the boom. If you're
angry at him, the phrase 'someday you'll understand' should be used frequently, as if you're
addressing a child."

Quite apart from the opportunity to display
your talent for delivering subtle or not-so-subtle
jabs, ditching by mail appears to have three obvious benefits: it costs just pennies; you don't have
to give a moment's thought to your appearance;
and you avoid confrontation.

We, however, cannot endorse this method.[1]
First of all, even the best writers tend to be too
flowery or over-the-top in such missives. One
woman we know, a very clever and talented writer,
came up with the following gem: "I am unwilling
to continue pouring the Dom Perignon of my heart
into the McDonald's giveaway cup of yours." In a
less emotionally fraught moment, she would have

---

[1]Which is not to say there is *no* place for letters in a breakup. Pre-ditch, writ-
ing a practice letter that you never send is a good exercise; it helps you sort
out your feelings and choose your words. And if you are breaking up with
a man you really do care for, a post-ditch letter that lists all the things you
genuinely like about him is sometimes a good idea. It reminds both of you
of what was valuable about the relationship.

been the first to recognize that such remarks should never find their way into print. She still cringes when she imagines him dining out on the story, regaling friends with tales about the crazy woman he dated, the one with the bloated prose.

Another significant drawback to this approach is its uncertainty. There is no way of knowing when the dumpee will actually receive, much less read, your epistle. "He was calling me saying, 'How are you, my love?' days after I'd sent it," says Pamela, who'd been going out with a man for almost a year when she fired off a letter telling him it was over. "Every time he phoned, I'd try to figure out from the tone of his 'hello' whether he'd got it yet."

Although many women believe this method to be clean, quick, and painless, it is not. "Since I sent it, it's all I've been thinking about," said Helen, the day after composing a letter to her long-distance lover. "Now it's in the mailbag, now it's on the plane, now it's probably slipping through his mail slot—you obsess about it constantly." And there's no sense of closure, for either of you. Frankly, we believe that any woman who thinks she won't drive herself crazy wondering how her victim is taking the news is in an advanced stage of denial.

Research shows that the kind of man most frequently ditched by mail is the Tin Man, and this is no coincidence. Whatever high-minded motive you may claim to have, the truth of the matter is that your letter is a last-ditch attempt to get his attention and provoke a response, preferably a grief-stricken one.

Let us be the first to tell you: it's not going to happen. The more likely scenario is that after a week or so of silence from his end, you decide to call him. Just to see how he's holding up. Here's how he answers the phone: "Hey! How ya doin'?" Music is blaring in the background, and you think you hear voices, too. Even though you've sworn to yourself that you absolutely will not mention the letter, you realize with horror that a voice is coming out of your mouth. It sounds out of control and very, very angry, and it's asking whether he ever had any intention of responding. He says, "Well, no." We can make only one guarantee about this conversation: at the end of it, you will feel as though *you've* been dumped.

Sometimes, of course, women choose the mail-order option simply because they dread confrontation. "I was afraid to tell Doug face to face," remembers Lisa, who had no sooner mailed her beau a "Dear John" letter than a friend reprimanded her for her poor form. "After two years, you owe him more than that," the friend declared. "He'll probably come over to your house after he gets the letter and bawl you out for not giving him an in-person explanation."

Consumed with guilt after this well-deserved tongue-lashing, Lisa left work early, dashed over to Doug's house, let herself in, and began rifling through his things, all the while praying he

---

ETIQUETTE TIPS

Dumping by Mail

The stationery of choice is the blank, unadorned note card, whose dimensions should not exceed 3" x 5". Printed messages and any illustrations, no matter how tasteful, are strictly forbidden. We insist on a small note card rather than loose paper because it ensures brevity; reams of foolscap will conjure images of a madwoman, we assure you.

The letter *must* be handwritten, not typed. And your spelling and grammar should be unassailable—his last memory of you should not be of a woman who splits her infinitives or is cavalier with a semicolon.

Choose your words carefully: you have no control over what he'll do with your letter after he receives it. Your missive may be passed around among his friends. Decades from now, it might turn up in his memoirs—or be unveiled when you run for political office.

When you have written the card and have read it over a dozen times, put it away for a minimum of forty-eight hours, during which time you are not to look at it even once. At the end of the waiting period, read it again with the cold eye of your worst enemy. Most likely, you will rip it up instantly and send us a thank-you letter, instead.

wouldn't come home and catch her trying to intercept his mail. But the letter hadn't been delivered yet, so she had to repeat this rigmarole for two more days. "When it finally arrived," says Lisa, "I shoved it in my purse and thanked God I'd had time to cool down and reconsider." That evening, she assuaged her guilt by doing the right thing: she took Doug out to a lovely French restaurant and dumped him over dinner.

Termination by facsimile

Upon hearing that one woman had dumped a boyfriend via facsimile, we dismissed the story as apocryphal. Sadly, we were mistaken. We have procured a copy of the fax and reprint the text here in its entirety: "Not coming for the weekend. And by the way, I think we should break up. Shelley."

It might seem that the fax is an improved version of the letter: one is far less tempted to go on at length, and the transmission is immediate. But we are dead set against this method: almost always, you will have to fax him at his office, so there's a good chance that others will see your memo before he does. In fact, you can never be sure that it will actually find its way to his desk.

Moreover, the fax is utterly devoid of class. "A fax shows she's in such a hurry, she can't even wait for the U.S. Postal Service—and is too cheap to buy a stamp," says Leonard.

Remember, you're gearing up for a public-relations battle, and the first salvo should not be aimed at your own foot. Your mutual friends will be horrified when they hear that you were so cold-hearted as to dump him via facsimile; even your own friends who say they think it's hilarious will have cause to reappraise your character.

There's just one exception to this embargo: if you're dating a workaholic who virtually lives at the office, and all other attempts to establish contact have failed.

ETIQUETTE TIPS

Dumping by Fax

As with the letter, so with the fax: it should be carefully worded and concise—three-quarters of a page, max.

The fax ditch must be preceded by a cover page, to reduce the likelihood that anyone else will read its contents. Under no circumstance should the cover page be marked "confidential," "top secret," or "urgent"— words that will undoubtedly pique widespread interest in his office.

Breaking up on the
information superhighway

If you meet a guy on the Web, why not dump him there, too? This was Sophie's reasoning. She was having an E-mail affair with a man who initially flooded her "In" box with messages every day. But after a few months, when they'd seen each other in the flesh on several occasions, the E-mails stopped coming quite as fast and furious, and their tone changed markedly. Where once they had been long and passionate, now they were terse and impersonal. Fortunately, Sophie recognized the signs: she knew it was time for a preemptive strike.

"I sent him an E-mail that mentioned everything from emotional damage to penis size," she recalls. "I felt totally in control and articulate—I'm sure if I'd had to speak to him, I would have been sputtering with rage. He E-mailed back insinuating that I was more into the relationship than he was, but I'd archived all his messages. I chose the mushiest one and sent it back to him for proof. That was the last I heard from him."

Before we even begin to analyze the efficacy of her method, we feel it necessary to point out that Sophie should count herself lucky. Most men you meet on the Internet are generally not there to engage in meaningful relationships. More likely, they're sixteen-year-old perverts who check into chat rooms only to take a short break from the arduous task of downloading pornography.

That being said, if you have become emotionally involved with a guy you met via computer, it is perfectly acceptable to get rid of him via the same medium. If, however, your relationship did not *begin* on the Internet, it's more than a little tacky to end it there. Not to mention risky: if you push the wrong button—or he does—your get-out-of-my-life E-mail could be circulating around the world.

ETIQUETTE TIPS

Dumping by E-mail

Above all, your E-mail ditch must be short. The dumpee shouldn't have to scroll through screens and screens of verbiage.

Text only, please. No musical accompaniments, dancing figures, sophisticated graphics, or deadly computer viruses are called for.

REACH OUT AND DUMP SOMEONE

The telephone might seem like your most convenient option. It's inexpensive, readily accessible, and requires much less effort than many other methods. It's also more democratic than, say, ditching via letter: the dumpee has an opportunity to say his piece. And it's more seemly than an in-person ditch, if your dumpee is given to bawling or shrieking.

"It's like a closed coffin, rather than an open one," explains Andrea, who has had great success with phone breakups. "Do you really want to see someone in that condition? And do they want to be seen?" And let's be honest: dumping by phone is "the easy way out if you're chicken."

It's perfectly fine to dump a guy by phone if you've only dated him once or twice—preferable, in fact, if your voice is deep, throaty, and pretty well your only outstanding attribute. The phone ditch is also an acceptable way to end a long-distance relationship, particularly if the unsuspecting dumpee is on the verge of booking an expensive plane ticket to come see you.

In almost all other situations, however, we have strong reservations about the dial-a-dump. For starters, there's a risk that the dumpee might misconstrue your meaning.[2] Second, because it's so

---

[2]The risk is especially great if you are one of those women who has in the past tried just about anything to prolong phone discussions. For example, when he said, "I've got to go," you tried to engage him in a Socratic dialogue. "I get the feeling you're trying to get rid of me. Which makes me wonder how much you really care about me. And if you don't care about

convenient, the phone is often used too impulsive-ly—after you've had a rough day at work, for example, and you're desperate to lash out at some-one. In this fevered state, you're unlikely to tell the dumpee in a calm, measured way that the relation-ship has come to an end; probably, you'll wind up declaring that you rue the day you met him.

Even when premeditated, ditching via phone is risky because it contains so many variables that cannot be controlled. Picture this: You've been preparing all day for your breakup. You've rehearsed your lines, but just in case, crib notes are by the phone. To guard against low blood sugar, you've eaten. A whole bag of ranch-flavor Doritos, in fact. You've created the perfect setting: Diet Coke and a box of Kleenex are within easy reach, and your friends are all on red alert for the postmortem calls.

You dial his number, but he answers, "I'm on the other line with work. I'll call you back."

This is fine, you tell yourself, it gives you the opportunity to run to the bathroom. And then the

me, why am I sleeping with you?" Such a woman will have a terrible time trying to convince her dumpee that she really means it when she announces, "It's over." Having developed an immunity to operatic declara-tions, he may well reply, "That's nice, sweetheart," and hang up with no inkling that he's now single.

kitchen, for more carbo-loading. Oh my God, there's the phone! "Hello?" you answer, a little breathlessly.

Oh. It's just one of your girlfriends, asking how the ditch went. You hustle her off the line: "He's calling back any second now."

Okay, sure, that threw you off a little, but it didn't derail you. You need some food to calm down. Oreos, perhaps. An hour passes. Then another. And another. Two friends call to say they can't wait any longer and are going to bed. Your grandmother is pissed as can be that you rushed her off the phone, at least according to your mother, who calls hourly to see if you've apologized yet.

By the time the prospective dumpee finally does get back to you, your whole mood has changed. Your heart's just not in it anymore. You feel so disgustingly fat, you're not sure you're in a position to be dumping *anyone* at this point. And somewhere along the line, you've misplaced the crib notes. Need we continue?

Even if you reach him right away and he's able to talk, many factors are still beyond your control. He could hang up, mid-ditch, before you've had a chance to finish your speech. This would be maddening. There's also a very strong possibility that

First and foremost, the dial-a-ditch is not a form of performance art. Chances are good, particularly if you are under the age of twenty, that your friends will beg to be present—or you will beg them to sit by your side, for moral support. But this is one call that you must make all on your own. If anyone else is in the room, you will almost certainly have a fit of the giggles.

Ignore call waiting entirely, even if it beeps nonstop—particularly if you're dumping a Reject Addict, whose ardor would only increase if you put him on hold.

A good rule of thumb: the length of a tele-ditch should not exceed the time required to travel by car from your house to his. If, for instance, the man lives around the corner and you can't be bothered to go over, you have no business spending hours on the phone analyzing the relationship. If, however, you're terminating a long-distance relationship, the conversation is unlikely to be short and sweet.

he won't believe you mean business until he sees your face, and will turn up at your door ten minutes later.

And one final word. About cell phones. If you call the dumpee while you're commuting and announce over a crackly line, "I've given it a lot of thought and want to end the relationship," he may doubt your protestations of grief and regret. There's a distinct lack of privacy, too: hundreds of people could be picking up snippets of your conversation. If you anticipate that he will make even one less than entirely flattering remark about you, it would be imprudent to proceed without a secure line. A woman we know, however, points out that cell phones do have one handy feature: "If he goes into weepy mode, you have the perfect and most polite exit strategy. Just say, 'I'm sorry, I'm going to lose you in a second—I'm heading into a tunnel.'"

AT THE SOUND OF THE TONE, DITCH HIM

Perhaps even a phone conversation is too frightening for you, so you're contemplating leaving a message on his answering machine. This method does have one advantage over all others: it's impossible to be long-winded—you'll be cut off automatically, usually after three or four minutes.

But anyone who is using this technique to end a long-term relationship ought to be ashamed of herself. Like Marcia, who'd been dating Harry for more than a year when she decided that the romance had stalled. "I was afraid Harry would say something to hurt me if he had the chance," she explains, "so I decided to leave a message on his office voice mail in the middle of the night. I should mention that this was also the night before I was leaving the country for three weeks. Anyway, I got into my nightgown and wrote out my main points on the back of an old envelope. I literally wrote out things like 'you're probably asleep now' in case I choked. My big line was something like, 'I don't want this to be bitter, it's just a sad thing. I'm gone and I'm not your girl-friend anymore.'"

We do recognize, however, that if you're dumping a Cling-on, you might have to make him despise you, in which case a voice-mail dump is ideal. Just ask Philippa. After their second date, Bruce sent her a note that said, "I'm not sure what's going on in our relationship and I need some reas-surance." She instantly recognized that she was dealing with a world-class Cling-on. "I had to do something extreme," she remembers. "So I called and left a message on his machine saying, 'May I suggest that in your next relationship, you refrain from sending wimpy little notes. They're a turnoff.' He never bothered me again."

Now, Philippa is British, and the Brits are known for tolerating absolutely no nonsense from Cling-ons. Of course, they are aided immensely by their clipped accents. Philippa's message would not have had the same impact had it been deliv-

Dumping by Answering Machine

A script is an absolute must, but it should never be obvious that you are reading from it. For example, "I really feel that you and I—*[long pause, during which sound of rustling paper is heard]*—do not belong—forever? No, wait, I think it says 'together.'"

If, midway through the ditch, you make a mistake—e.g., sneeze, or say something nice—many voice-mail systems will allow you to erase your message and start over *as long as you don't hang up first.*

To ensure that your voice sounds strong and confident, take a few minutes to breathe deeply before dialing his number. Place your hand on your stomach, inhale until your diaphragm expands to full capacity, hold your breath for a count of five, then slowly exhale; repeat ten times. Warning: *do not look down while performing this exercise*—the sight of your own distended abdomen will throw you off.

ered with flat or nasal vowels. Most North American women simply can't make a voice-mail ditch sound definitive enough to scare off a Cling-on, which is why, reluctantly, we restrict our endorsement of this method to women born within the United Kingdom.

Even there, however, a large proportion of the population is voice-mail challenged; many highly articulate individuals turn into stammering ninnies as soon as they hear the phrase, "After the tone, please leave a message." If you have left a rambling, incoherent message even once in your life, you should not be considering this method—nothing is more of a turn-on for a Cling-on than a discombobulated woman.

———

So what technique gets our unconditional seal of approval?

The in-person breakup, naturally. Read on.

CHAPTER EIGHT

Expiration Dates

Ideal Locations for Your Last Rendezvous

Really, only one breakup method is above reproach: the face-to-face ditch. As etiquette doyenne Letitia Baldrige once put it, "The person doing the walking has a responsibility to show as much compassion as possible." Showing compassion means giving the dumpee a cathartic opportunity to say his piece—*in person.* An in-person ditch accords him the respect he deserves, and ensures that both of you have a sense of closure. If you ever had any feelings for this man, you owe him at least that much.

Besides, if you try to terminate the romance in absentia, he'll almost certainly find a way to see you one last time. He might turn up unexpectedly at an inopportune moment—say, when your new love is stealing away from your home at dawn's early light. Therefore, it's best for all concerned if you do the right thing: dump him in person.

Remember, only if you absolutely couldn't change your schedule would you skip an office party or a friend's wedding shower. So please, make every reasonable effort to attend your own breakup.

On the menu tonight, we have . . . your breakup!

The restaurant breakup is an obsessive-compulsive's dream, but everyone else's worst nightmare: even if you plan meticulously, something unexpected could happen and the whole operation could be botched. For example, a street vendor could appear table-side, pre-ditch, and harangue the dumpee into buying "roses for the lovely lady." To reduce the possibility of such calamities, observe the following *Do's* and *Don'ts*.

Do choose a restaurant with the appropriate ambience. A popular one will be too noisy and crowded. If, on the other hand, the restaurant is deserted, there will be insufficient background noise and every word you say will reverberate through the room; busboys with nothing else to do will hover obtrusively. Last but not least, the place must be within your own means—there's a very strong possibility the dumpee won't be picking up the check.

Don't select an eatery that has figured in your history with the dumpee. It's well-nigh impossible to focus on your breakup when you're being mobbed by adoring waiters clamoring to have a word with "our favorite couple."

Don't pick a place that's highly recommended by friends or coworkers. Picture this: Someone from your office suddenly materializes at the next table, just as your dumpee is launching into a full-scale character assassination. Or, while he's fighting back tears, someone he knows shows up and bellows, "So I finally get to meet the love of your life!" If you see anyone either of you knows in the restaurant before you've initiated the breakup, abort the mission immediately. If the breakup is already in progress, try to wrap it up as quickly as possible.

Don't go to a restaurant that's had sensational reviews. The food should be unexceptional; solemnly announcing, "There's something missing from our relationship," then involuntarily blurting, "Oh my God, this double-chocolate torte is to die for," is *most* inappropriate. Laurie learned this lesson the hard way, when she dumped a guy at an upscale Japanese restaurant. "The sushi was so fabulous that I couldn't work up the right display of emotions," she recalls. "I was trying to be serious and sympathetic, but meanwhile, I was cramming sushi into my mouth, saying, 'If you're not going to finish, can I have yours, too?' He was so shaken, he couldn't eat a thing, so I cleaned both our plates. He was appalled, and I have to admit, it did kind of interfere with the gravity of the situation."

Do visit the restaurant beforehand. It's a good idea to work out a prearranged signal with the waiter so that he will bring you the check on cue, rather than keeping a diplomatic distance because your dinner companion is sobbing inconsolably. Familiarize yourself with the location of *all* exits, since trying to make a quick getaway in a restaurant laid out like a warren is difficult at the best of times. Besides, knowing the lay of the land will reinforce your sense of being in control.

Do choose your table carefully. Ideally, it should be at least three feet away from other diners, to minimize eavesdropping, and within sight of the door.

Don't check your coat. However, strongly encourage him to check his. This will insure that you have a head start if it becomes imperative to flee.

Don't drink and ditch. Slurred exit lines are never as effective, especially when they're delivered to a half-crocked dumpee.

As for the specific timing of your announcement, think of it as a toast of sorts (although no clinking of glasses is necessary): it should be delivered after the main course is finished and the plates have been cleared. Introducing the topic at the beginning of a four-course meal is a recipe for a protracted argument, not to mention indigestion, and it allows your dinner guest too many opportunities to weaken your resolve.

All this planning might sound like far too much trouble, but with a Cling-on, the extra effort is well worth it. For one thing, the management will impose a time limit on your last rendezvous: after a few hours, they'll insist that you free up the table. A helpful hint: if your Cling-on is vehemently anti-tobacco, arrange to sit in the smoking section—and, if necessary, puff away madly on the most noxious cigarettes you can lay your hands on. It will shorten the ordeal considerably.

A restaurant may be your *only* breakup venue

option if you're getting rid of a Sexual Savant. A little-known law governs the termination of purely physical liaisons: the number of times per day you fantasize about him, multiplied by twenty, equals the number of yards that must be between you and a bed, any bed, when you ditch him.

Linda thought she could break this law with impunity but soon discovered otherwise. "Every time I tried to break up with him at his place, I'd wind up thinking, 'I'll just sleep with him this one last time,'" says Linda, who was dating a man she describes as "an anatomical phenomenon, like something out of *National Geographic.*" Before long, she realized she'd have to dump him in a location where there was absolutely no risk that she'd give in to her own desires.

For a Garden-Variety Man, however, the restaurant ditch is not recommended: it's far too public, and not nearly respectful enough. Even if the subject of your relationship comes up one night when you're out for dinner and he asks point-blank whether you're thinking about leaving him, practice restraint. Wait until you've left the restaurant and can have a real conversation in a private place where there are no spectators.

Breaking up on a budget

If you're looking for a bargain, the park can be a very attractive venue. "It's private, but also public," says Julie. "There's pretty scenery and plenty of fresh air. There's something kind of romantic about it, actually. I've broken up with tons of guys in parks."

The park is also brimming with metaphorical significance: without saying a word, you're able to suggest that breaking up is as natural as your surroundings. If he has even the most cursory knowledge of semiotics, the subtext won't be lost on him.

But if the truth be told, the park is a little *too* natural for our liking. Let's face it, the elements can play havoc with your appearance. What if, midditch, the clouds open and your hair goes frizzy—then flat? Even Julie concedes there are risks: "One time, a wasp started buzzing around my head. It was distracting, swatting at it and trying to be serious at the same time."

A word of caution about island getaways. Most metropolitan areas boast a large patch of nature which can only be reached by seafaring vehicle. You may be thinking, "Well, that qualifies as a park." Technically, you are right. But when it comes to your breakup, the island park is also the ninth circle of hell. *There is no quick way to get back to the mainland—for either of you.*

If you remain unconvinced, imagine how *you* would feel if you were whisked off to an island for what you believed to be a fun-filled day trip, only to be dumped unceremoniously. For one of us— we can't say which one (all right, it was Kate)—no imagination is required. *This actually happened.* The man in question lured her to an island park located ninety minutes from her home. He went so far as to instruct her to bring a bathing suit. No sooner had they disembarked from the ferry— which, by the by, promptly sailed off, leaving her stranded for a full hour—than he casually announced that he had no intention of continuing their involvement.

It doesn't matter what he's done to you or how much you hate him. Disposing of him at an island park is beyond the pale.

ASSUME THE CRASH POSITION

An airport is one of the most dramatic backdrops for a breakup. Even if you're at O'Hare rather than a deserted landing strip à la *Casablanca,* there's something undeniably cinematic about jettisoning a man before boarding a plane.

The airport also ranks high in terms of practicality. There are plenty of people around but most of them live elsewhere, so if something embarrassing transpires, no one you know will hear about it unless you choose to tell all. And tears are far less conspicuous here than, say, in a restaurant; misty-eyed couples are a standard feature of any airport.

Best of all, there's a built-in escape route: you're getting on a plane. The fact that you're flying off to another city gives you the sense of a new beginning, even if you're just going home. You feel unencumbered and ready to move on. The dumpee, too, has a sense of finality. You're out of his life not just figuratively, but literally.[1]

If you are planning an airport ditch, call ahead to confirm that your flight is on schedule. If by chance your flight is delayed when you're already at the airport, complete your breakup as planned and proceed immediately through the security checkpoint. At most airports, the dumpee can't follow you unless he has a boarding pass, and you can always reemerge when you're certain the coast is clear. One last thought: if you find yourself

---

[1] If he's the one getting on a plane, however, an airport ditch can backfire rather spectacularly. He might refuse to leave, and you could be stuck with him for days while he tries to convince you to reconsider.

weeping, do not panic and try to brush the tears away—they can be useful in securing a free upgrade to first class.

Turn out the lights, the party's over

An alarming number of breakups occur at parties. This is not altogether surprising, since it is often at a social gathering that it dawns on you that a) you're interested in another man, b) you're certainly not interested in the man you're with, or c) both of the above. This epiphany can lead to some unplanned but nonetheless riveting entertainment for the rest of the guests. Nothing makes a soirée quite so memorable as a messy public breakup that involves one party sobbing in the bathroom while the other shouts obscenities through the locked door.

One woman of our acquaintance mesmerized a huge crowd when she very publicly dumped her date at a large, formal gathering. No one knew the cause of the rupture or whether she had been provoked. All anyone knew was that he remained at their table, slack-jawed, as she sashayed around the dance floor like a shameless strumpet, flinging herself at any man who crossed her path. In case you didn't guess from the previous sentence, this woman did irreversible damage to her reputation.

Which is why we are adamant: *never*—no matter how profound the distaste for your soon-to-be ex-beau—dump a guy at a party. We do not care if the dumpee bores everyone to tears with stories about his office capers. We do not even care if he becomes hideously drunk and announces to all and sundry that you slept with him on the first date.

If you rebuff him in front of other people, *your* conduct, not his, will become the focus of attention. Instead, shock them with your seemingly generous spirit and limitless understanding. While you seethe internally, silently chant your mantra: *There's always tomorrow.* Besides, it's better to ditch him when he's sober enough to appreciate your withering indictment of his character.

YOUR PLACE OR MINE?

If your relationship is at all serious, chances are good that you'll want to end it in the privacy of your own home. But frankly, we think that your place, lovely though it may be, is a terrible breakup spot. He might overstay his welcome, and if either of you is a screamer or a weeper, an at-home ditch could disturb the neighbors.

Breaking up at his place, on the other hand, is a fine idea. Before you begin your good-bye speech, you can casually amble around, stuffing your purse with any items you've been unable to retrieve on previous missions. It's also kinder to him to do it on his turf: he might derive immense satisfaction from doing something dramatic, like yelling, "Get out, right now!" Which, let's face it, dovetails nicely with your plans.

If you've made the mistake of moving in together, remember the golden rule: if *you're* dumping *him,* no matter what the provocation, you must be prepared to leave the abode you share, at least temporarily, immediately post-ditch. We can imagine few things more hypocritical than crawling into bed with a man mere hours after telling him the relationship is over.

———

But enough minor details. Now that you've selected the location, it's time to move on to the really important issue: what are you going to wear?

CHAPTER NINE

What Should
I Wear?
Dressing for Ditching

You would never dream of dressing
down for a first date, a job interview, or
a party. Yet many women do just that
for their breakups. Some think that,
since the relationship is about to be over, it hardly
matters what they wear. Others believe it's possible
to alleviate the dumpee's misery by looking less
than entirely appealing. Whatever the rationale,
turning up ill-attired for an expiration date is a
grievous error.

Looking bad *doesn't* soften the blow. And, as
long as there is any possibility whatsoever that you
might encounter another living soul mid-dump,
you must dress like the woman you truly are: one
who will be on the market again in approximately
five minutes.

Most important, it's crucial to feel you have the
upper hand at your breakup, and looking your

best certainly helps. When you look good, you feel more confident—and even if you *don't* feel confident, well, at least you look good.

The amount of time you spend on your appearance on the Big Day should be inversely proportional to the strength of the dumpee's devotion. Thus, breaking up with a Tin Man requires the most preparation. You don't just want to look attractive when you ditch him—you want to look sensational. But, we hasten to add, *not* drop-dead sexy; you do not want to leave him with the impression that you're still frantically trying to lure him into bed. Instead, think timeless elegance. Think Audrey Hepburn. Think, in short, about booking ahead with a good hairdresser.

"The goal is to create a lasting impression that haunts all his future girlfriends," says Erica. "If there's time, I may even go and get my hair hennaed a few days before." (N.B., dyes, rinses, and perms generally look best after a week; ditto with facials. Do not let a rogue beauty professional intimidate you into one or more of these procedures on the day of your breakup.)

Even with a Cling-on, your appearance should be a priority. This might seem illogical. After all, this is the hardest breed to dump, and your first instinct is to do everything in your power to repel him. But you don't need to dress down to make your dumpee dislike you—you can be plenty unpleasant in Armani. Fur, however, is a no-no. You shouldn't wear anything that might attract protesters.

Do wear something that makes you feel comfortable—and would not in any way impede you from sprinting down the street should it become necessary to make a quick getaway. Nothing fussy, since you might not have time to struggle with a row of tiny buttons or yank at a stubborn zipper. Bulky knapsacks, beach totes, and gym bags should be left at home—heavy bags will only slow you down. If you don't have one already, this is the time to invest in a small clutch.[1]

Accessories should be kept to a bare minimum. You don't want to be scrabbling around on the floor trying to find a missing glove, and God forbid you should have to go back to retrieve it. Dark glasses, though, are a nice touch, enabling you to hide your tears. Or lack thereof. A watch, too, can be helpful: you can consult it if the breakup drags on and on, affect a look of horror, and say, "Oh no,

---

[1]It should, however, be big enough to contain a breakup survival kit, which includes the following: safety pins, extra panty hose, tissues, Visine, breath mints, hairbrush, and, depending on your dumpee, either Valium or earplugs.

I had to be somewhere fifteen minutes ago!"

Other jewelry should be selected with the utmost caution. *Never* wear an item he has given you. You may entertain the fantasy that you will offer to return this love token, whereupon he will tearfully insist that you keep it as a memento. Well, our sources tell us that such dramatic gestures often backfire. Upon presentation, one man we know calmly flushed his girlfriend's cherished trinkets down the toilet. Only one piece of jewelry *must* be returned: an engagement ring.

Hosiery, while not mandatory, should always be black—the most slimming color currently available. White stockings have the opposite effect and thus are absolutely forbidden at your breakup (and, for that matter, at any other time).

Sadly, many women who spend a great deal of time and energy putting together a lovely breakup trousseau neglect their footwear. If there is just one thing we can impress upon you, let it be this: flats are the sine qua non for a breakup. His final memory of you should not be of a woman wobbling down the street in six-inch heels, clutching onto parking meters for support.

Remember: *you never have a second chance to make a last impression.*

CHAPTER TEN

We Have to Talk …

Exit Lines

Composing the farewell speech is by far the most difficult part of the breakup ordeal. Many cowards find it *so* difficult that they give up and decide to wing it, figuring that the right words will magically come to them when they're face to face with the dumpee. The results are usually disastrous: they become so nervous that they ramble incoherently, say something hurtful, and/or leave the dumpee with the mistaken impression that the relationship is still going strong.

Your breakup is not the time to practice your extemporaneous speaking skills. It is the time to stick to your script, which should be worked out well in advance, committed to memory, and rehearsed in front of a mirror. You should know it so well that you could recite it in your sleep.

The most critical element of your speech is, of

course, the exit line: the key reason you are offering to the dumpee for ending the relationship. If
you've only gone out a few times, you want to be
tactful yet firm. If you're ending a serious relationship, you don't want to hurt his feelings, nor do
you want to insult his intelligence with clichés.
Following, a cornucopia of some of the best—and
worst—parting lines known to womankind.

Elements *of a* Good Exit Line

- *It doesn't hurt the dumpee gratuitously*

- *It is convincing*

- *It is irrefutable*

- *It gives him no reason to believe you'll change your mind*

- *It doesn't sound hackneyed*

- *It does not harm your own reputation—no one to whom he repeats it will think less of you*

- *It can be delivered with a straight face*

Rejecting a guy after just a few dates

"I don't have time for a relationship right now. I'm just too busy."

Everyone knows that when you're really interested, you *make* the time. Thus, only women who are extraordinarily busy—medical residents and interns, jet-setting executives, etc.—have any hope of pulling this off. In all other cases, the dumpee will a) know you're lying, or b) counter, "Can't we still see each other, just less frequently?"

"Don't take this personally. It's not you, it's me."

Not only unoriginal but nonsensical: when you ditch a guy, of course he takes it personally.

"I'm moving."

If you have no mutual friends, are absolutely certain you'll never bump into the dumpee again, and are prepared to get a new, unlisted phone number, this is an excellent excuse. The only other circumstance under which it should be used is if you *are* in fact moving. Parenthetically, we should note that some women actually do move solely to get rid of unwanted beaux; although this seems a bit extreme, they insist it's a delightful way to see the world.

"A friend of mine—I'm not at liberty to say who—told me she's secretly in love with you, and would never forgive me if I saw you again."

Top marks for creativity. You look like a loyal—and remarkably discreet—friend. And rather than feeling rejected, the dumpee feels like a sex object, and spends a pleasant week or two fantasizing about the mystery woman. But around week three, he'll start pressing you for clues to her identity, and demand to know why, if she loves him so much, she's not willing to declare herself. In short, he'll be pestering you for some time to come.

"I'm a little confused about my sexual orientation."

If true, this is unbeatable. And even if not, this line can work wonders, according to one of our sources. She and a friend went carousing one night and spent a pleasant few hours dancing wildly with two gentlemen; at the end of the evening, it became clear that the men had romantic expectations that the women had no intention of fulfilling. So, after a brief conference in the bathroom, they emerged and declared, "Thank you, this has been such an *unusual* evening for us. But now, we hope you don't mind if we dance this last slow one together." As they embraced on the dance floor, the men ran for the exit. We applaud this piece of feminine ingenuity, but caution the rest of you: use this excuse only if you're certain you'll never run into the dumpee again—and if you're positive he won't say, "Cool! Can I watch?"

"Trust me, I'm so screwed up, you really don't want to be with me."

Very unconvincing, as Ellen discovered the hard way. Her dumpee thought "screwed up" meant "really deep" (which, in Ellen's case, it does not) and took this line as a challenge. If you want to drive him away, merely telling him you're a wacko won't do the trick. You have to *show* him . . .

"My other personality, Sally, doesn't like you."

Much better, but very difficult to execute. But if you *can* say this without laughing, your dumpee will run for the hills. And don't worry about negative PR: if he tells others that you have a multiple personality disorder, they'll think *he's* out of his mind.

"You're so great that I couldn't just have a casual relationship with you. But at this point in my life, I can't handle anything serious."

To you, this might seem downright complimentary; you're implying that you have too much respect for your dumpee to engage in anything but an epic romance with him. But if the dumpee believes you're sincere, he's likely to lurk around, hoping that one day you *will* be ready for a serious relationship. Alternatively, if he's sharp-witted, he'll divine your true meaning—not only do you not want a relationship, you can't even bear the thought of a fling—and be mortally offended.

"A friend of mine just told me she gives blow jobs—isn't that disgusting?*"*

Nothing short of brilliant. If you ever lay eyes on him again, we'll be mighty surprised.

"I really value our friendship, and I don't want to risk losing it by getting romantically involved."

Oh, please! When there's even the slightest sexual spark, the average woman couldn't care less about risking a friendship. However, if you don't think your dumpee will figure out that you're blathering on in this insufferably high-minded fashion because you're simply not attracted to him, go right ahead and use this line. But rethink the friendship—he sounds like a moron.

"I just don't feel I can be in a sexual relationship right now."

Almost always uttered after days or weeks of fooling around with the dumpee, this really means,

"I'm wearying of sex with *you*." Astonishingly, however, many men fall for it, because they believe sex is never just *sex* to women, it always has powerful spiritual and emotional significance. To which we say: why tell them the truth, if it means robbing ourselves of such a great exit line?

"You've got to respect a guy like the Unabomber."

Just one example of a whole genre of exit lines geared toward offending the dumpee so deeply that he can't in good conscience spend another minute with you. By figuring out what's abhorrent to him—maybe it's a political issue, maybe a religious conviction—you can come up with a line to suit your own needs. A cautionary note: this approach should be used only as a last resort, because your outrageous remark(s) will most assuredly become public knowledge.

"I thought I was ready for a relationship, but I was wrong. I haven't recovered from the last one."

Yes, you come off looking rather noble, like the kind of woman who doesn't just hop from one guy to the next. But there are serious drawbacks. The dumpee might tell everyone that you're still obsessively fixated on your last boyfriend, thereby discouraging other men from asking you out.

"Things are getting serious with a man I started dating just before I met you, and it wouldn't be right for me to see you anymore."

Our favorite for short-term liaisons. Whether or not you're bluffing, you come off looking like a Nice Girl who would never consider anything except strict monogamy. Moreover, he's unlikely to take the rejection personally: another man was ahead of him in line, that's all. Our sources tell us that the dumpee sometimes even says, with charming naïveté, "Well, if it doesn't work out with him, give me a call."

ENDING A FULL-FLEDGED RELATIONSHIP

"I need some space right now."

Disastrously gradual. It's cruel to give him reason to believe that your parting is only temporary, and it's not in your own self-interest, either. At some point, you'll have to lower the boom—why not do it right now?

"I love you too much—it scares me."

An ingenious way to rid yourself of a man with an enormous ego, since he's highly susceptible to the notion that he makes women feel dangerously out of control. But to clinch the deal, you might need to add a coda: "Please don't phone me or try to see me again—ever. I'm just not strong enough to resist the temptation."

"You're too possessive for me."

Our all-time favorite for a Tin Man, who is, of course, anything but possessive. Even if he is aware that he's been emotionally distant, this line will confuse him no end, and will make you feel much better.

"I could never make you happy long-term."

Problematic, since the dimmer dumpee might not even recognize that you're trying to cut him loose. "But you *do* make me happy!" he might bray. "Hon, don't be so hard on yourself!"

"Let's get married."

Can be an effective faux excuse. Many a man bows out quickly when he learns that a woman is hell-bent on domesticating him. But never, ever deliver this line to a Cling-on or Lapdog, either of whom might reply, "Great! Let's set a date."

"You don't make enough money."

Effective in one respect: he'll be thankful you're dumping him after you utter these words. But the

What to Expect When You're Rejecting

Don't make the mistake of thinking that you can make your dumpee agree that it would be better if the two of you parted ways. If he really likes you, it doesn't matter how many sound reasons you present—he still won't think that being ditched is good for him. In fact, you should expect the dumpee to challenge your decision. But you'll be able to hold your own in a debate if you know your cues.

When He Says . . .	You Should Say . . .
What about all those times you told me you loved me? Didn't you mean it?	Of course I meant it. But my feelings have changed.
Is the problem that you're not sexually attracted to me?	Of course not. There's certainly no lack of chemistry between us. (Say this even if it's a complete lie—it will make him feel much, much better.)
Nobody will ever love you the way I do.	You may be right.
I'll change.	It wouldn't make any difference. I've already made up my mind.
You led me on.	Everything I said and did I meant at the time.

When He Says . . .	You Should Say . . .
Let's go for counseling together and try to work this out.	There would be no point. I've given this decision a lot of thought, and nothing is going to change my mind.
How long have you been feeling this way?	Not long. But long enough to know I'm making the right decision.
Is there someone else?	No. This is about you and me.
I guess I'm just not good enough for you.	I don't think this relationship is good for either of us.
Do you think you'll want to get back together at some point in the future?	Not in the foreseeable future, no.
How could you do this to me?	I'm sorry if you feel I've misled you, and I really regret hurting you.
I can't live without you.	Sometimes I feel that way about you, too. It's going to be hard for both of us, but I know it's the right decision.
Was it something I did?	This isn't about one specific incident; I just don't think this relationship is going anywhere.
Does this mean we're never going to see each other again?	At least not for a while. It would just make it harder for both of us to move on.

PR implications are grave indeed. It's fine to think that a wealthy man would be more to your liking, but you should *never* say so out loud.

"I don't love you. Even though I've told you in the past that I loved you, I don't think I ever really did."

First-rate, if your goal is to make him—and everyone he knows—despise you. You may be horrified now that you ever did care for the dumpee, but it is reprehensible to deny history. And if you're not denying history, this line makes you look like an idiot: why were you telling a guy you loved him when you didn't? "We've grown apart" will suffice.

"I love you, but I'm not in love with you."

Crushing. In essence, you're saying you think of him as a brother—an idea that's repellent to most dumpees. In fact, they often argue: "You're confusing true love with infatuation. Love lasts a lifetime—'in love' is always fleeting."

"I want to become more Catholic, and I need to be with a man who shares my faith."

Sure to scare the hell out of a non-Catholic. Another plus: it allows the dumpee to depart with his ego intact. He'll reason that the breakup has nothing to do with him—it's all part of a plan that God cooked up. Moreover, announcing that you're on a religious bender makes you seem pure and honorable, yet considerably less appealing (any day now, you might decide to swear off premarital sex). If your dumpee doesn't pick up on the implication, spell it out: "Oh, and by the way, I'm giving up sex for Lent."

"I could never marry someone who isn't Jewish."

Another winner, even if you *aren't* Jewish. This line suggests that you think so highly of him that you would consider marriage, if only he were of the right religious persuasion. Should he offer to convert, simply say, "I couldn't allow it. You'd only wind up resenting me."

"There's someone else."

It's a little late for a policy of total honesty. After all, you've been sneaking around on the dumpee—or contemplating it—for weeks or even months now. Besides, the new man is not the *cause* of the breakup; you wouldn't have gone on the prowl unless there was something wrong with your relationship to begin with. So spare the dumpee the details of your infidelities, and pick a more generic exit line.

TROUBLESHOOTING GUIDE

My dumpee doesn't speak English fluently—what's the best exit line?

The simplest one. Learn from Joanne's mistake. She had to ditch a Frenchman, and composed a speech complete with flowery phrases and subtle nuances. "After I told him, I felt so relieved. I said, 'So, you understand, then?'" she recalls. "He said, '*Non.* Please to repeat again more slow.' I did, but he still didn't get it. In the end, I practically had to mime the breakup: 'You'—'Me'—'Fini.'"

What if my dumpee agrees that breaking up is a good idea, and doesn't seem heartbroken at all?

Even though this is a blow to your ego, it definitely means that you've made the right decision. Don't do what Tina did. So eager was she to get rid of her dumpee that she'd already arranged to get back together with her old boyfriend. But when she announced her plans, her dumpee "agreed to the breakup so cheerfully that it made me feel that *I'd* been ditched," she says. "I made a complete fool of myself trying to get him back, and by the time I came to my senses, another woman had already snapped up my old boyfriend."

What if my dumpee says or does something while I'm ditching him that makes me reconsider?

Stay the course. Most cowards have spent weeks or months weighing the pros and cons of a ditch; no one can say your decision was hasty, and you should not reverse it in the heat of the moment. Natalie once made this error and lived to regret it. She was dumping a guy primarily because they had never had a good conversation when, mid-ditch, he delivered a spellbinding oration. "We wound up talking all night, and by the end of the evening, we were back together," she remembers. "I was all excited: the ditch had actually brought us closer together, and now we'd have fabulous conversations all the time. That turned out to be the first and last good discussion we ever had."

What should I do if my dumpee clams up while I'm ditching him?

Silence is your friend. Long pauses are to be expected during your breakup, and the worst thing you could do is try to fill them. If you begin improvising, you are likely to say too much. Stick to your script.

I can't bring myself to say any of these lines. Isn't there a backup plan for the incurable coward?

Yes, in fact, there is! Casually leave a copy of this book where the dumpee will see it, and highlight the following passage: *I don't want to see you anymore— please go away.*

"I'm not happy. I've given this a lot of thought, and I know I won't be happy. I think we should break up.

Our favorite for terminating longer-term relationships, because it's definitive and honest, yet artfully vague. Other benefits: you're not attacking the dumpee, and you needn't be a trained thespian to deliver this line (though squeezing out a few crocodile tears certainly wouldn't hurt). Of course, you may be asked why, exactly, you're unhappy, in which case the correct response is, "There's no single reason, it's just a general feeling." If your dumpee persists in demanding a specific reason, simply repeat your exit line, over and over: "Look, I've given this a lot of thought, and I'm just not happy." After he's heard this thirty or forty times, he'll get bored and go home.

CHAPTER ELEVEN

OK, OK, I Slept with Your Brother...

But Can't We Still Be Friends?

Immediately after delivering the sad news, it's not uncommon for a woman to add what she believes is an inspired flourish: she leans over, gently touches the arm of the man whose heart she's just stomped on, and says in her most sympathetic tone, "I really hope we can still be friends."

"That ought to cheer him up a bit!" she thinks. "He hasn't lost me forever—he's only had his bedroom privileges revoked." Proffering the olive branch seems like the civilized thing to do: after all, the dumpee has a number of redeeming qualities—it would be ridiculous *not* to be friends with him. Besides, if she changes her mind, it will be

easier to get the dumpee back if they're still hanging around together.

Even if you've done something unspeakable to
him, you too will be tempted to say, "Let's be
friends." It's an instinctive female reflex—and one
you must suppress.

To begin with, the dumpee is rarely overjoyed
to be offered a consolation prize. In fact, he usually says something prickly, like, "Thanks, but I
already have plenty of friends." This reaction is
hardly surprising. In essence, he's just been told by
a woman he's attracted to that she likes everything
about him—except the prospect of any further
physical contact. Moreover, even the least astute
dumpee knows that it would be painful to hang
around by the stage door while his ex holds cast-
ing calls for his replacement.

Sometimes, however, a particularly love-struck
dumpee *will* agree to be "just friends," but only
because he believes it's his best chance to win you
back. At first, it might seem that the imbalance in
your affections doesn't matter, but after a while, it
will start to annoy you that he's forever suggesting
that you take your shirt off so he can give you a
"friendly back rub."

Furthermore, you'll tire of having to censor

yourself. "You have to pretend you feel like shit because of the breakup, even though you don't," Patty says. "After I dumped James, he'd call and say, 'How are you?' I'd have to say, 'How could I be? It's really rough. I take each day as it comes.' Meanwhile, I was dating like crazy." Trying to be friends isn't just hard on him, it's hard on *you*. You wind up having to reject his overtures again and again, which just makes you feel worse.

None of this is to say that you should be *un*friendly should your paths cross after the breakup, just that both of you should be moving on. As Sari says, "My policy is no phone calls, no mercy visits, no follow-up conversations. It's cruel to keep him hanging on—you're just trying to feed your ego and make sure he still likes you. If you really do want to break up, it's unfair to send him mixed signals. If you feel sad and lonely some night, call your mother, your friend, that guy who likes you—anyone but your ex."

At this point, you might be saying, "But I was friends with him beforehand—surely that means I can be friends with him now." No doubt, before hormones took over, the two of you had some angst-ridden, terribly earnest discussions about not wanting to endanger the friendship. Back then, you knew you were risking something—and you were right.

It's possible that you may be friends with your dumpee at some point in the future, but it won't be soon, and it won't be at your instigation. *He* is the one who has to make the overtures—and you shouldn't accept them until his wounds have healed and you could have something approaching an equal friendship.

DIVIDING THE FAMILY JEWELS

If it's been a long-term relationship, you may be wondering: What about other members of his family? Am I supposed to cut *them* off, too?

The very idea upsets you. What tragic fate would befall his little sister, the one who idolizes you? In her formative years, it could be most damaging for her to lose her role model through no fault of her own. And what about his older brother, the one with the generous employee discount at Banana Republic? You can't possibly give them up!

And why should you? Staying in touch with his family will actually make matters better for *him*; they're going to be upset enough as it is that he's botched yet another relationship. Plus, if you stick around, you'll be better able to preserve their good opinion of you. The dumpee might let it slip, for example, that you cheated on him before you got around to ending the relationship. If you're still in the picture, being your old goody-two-shoes self, they'll be less likely to believe such allegations.

It's perfectly understandable that you don't want to sever ties with his family. But consider, for a moment, the dumpee. He should not have to compete with you for the affections of his nearest and dearest. Take it from George, who found himself in this predicament after being dumped by his longtime girlfriend, Kim. "I expected my family to join me in a total freeze-out," he says. "But my mother said, 'This is between you and Kim,' and she kept in touch with her. On a primitive level, it's a massive betrayal. You think, 'Hey, whose team are you on?'"

Now, the dumpee might actually *encourage* you to continue seeing his family. "Of course I wanted her to stay in touch with them," says Ken. "When someone you love leaves, you'll do *anything* to keep her in your orbit. You'd sell your best friend down the river if it would help." In other words, a brokenhearted dumpee is not a good judge of what's in his best interests. You, therefore, must act *in loco parentis.*

Let's face facts: the dumpee's pain will not be alleviated if his mother is going out for cozy little lunches with you and returning with tales about your new and improved love life. But it won't be her fault. It will be *yours*, for putting her in such an untenable position.

Surely the most outrageous example we've heard concerns a woman we'll call "Penny." After beginning a steamy fling with another man, she dumped her beloved in a long, drawn-out fashion seemingly designed to exact the maximum amount of suffering. Shortly thereafter, she mailed off a birthday card to his mother, enclosing a thoughtful little note intended to tug at her heartstrings. Understandably, the dumpee went ballistic when his mother innocently mentioned that she had received a very sweet message from the unfailingly considerate Penny. He couldn't vent his rage on the perpetrator, so he gave his poor, blameless mother a tongue-lashing, instead. Penny, if you're reading this, please stop with the birthday cards.

Ending a relationship entails certain sacrifices, not the least of which is contact with his family. As Denise puts it, "It's kind of selfish to say, 'Look, you can have your toothbrush back, but I'm keeping your Mom.'" Besides, *you* need to get on with your life. You might think, immediately post-ditch, that you have no feelings for him whatsoever. But if you hear three months later that he has a new girlfriend and the family "just loves her," you may feel a twinge of regret—or murderous rage. Rest assured that your replacement will be less than thrilled to learn that her boyfriend's ex is still part of the family, and may kick up quite a fuss (as would you, if the tables were turned). Ultimately, his family will think less of you for putting them in such an awkward position.

Anyway, you should be putting your energies into more important things: namely, winning over your new boyfriend's relatives.

CHAPTER TWELVE

Encore! Encore!
Or, Sex with the Ex?

Now that you've accepted that you can't be friends with your dumpee, at least not for a while, you might be pondering the philosophical question that has perplexed women for millennia: is it permissible to have sex with the dumpee one last time? You may, upon reflection, come to the conclusion that ruling out friendship does not mean ruling out sex. After all, you're not in the habit of sleeping with your friends.

Some women, in fact, heartily endorse post-ditch sex and believe it is the ultimate erotic experience. There's the delicious uncertainty—is he still game?—and a stirring conviction: you're not just making love, you're making *history* (this is, you tell yourself, *definitely* the last time).

Unlike sex with a new partner, sex with an ex does not entail any awkward conversations about HIV status or birth control. Nor is there the shyness about physical imperfections that generally accompanies the inaugural disrobing. The dumpee knows perfectly well what your body looks like, and is delighted to be viewing it again. Best of all you do not have to suffer in silence or issue detailed instructions if his technique is less than satisfactory. He already knows what works for you, and on this particular occasion, he'll be going for broke.

Given these benefits, we can certainly understand the temptation to have one last tango with the dumpee. But try to resist, because while the sex might be great, the consequences are usually quite unpleasant.

One or both of you might burst into tears. You may think you no longer have an emotional attachment to the dumpee, so sex with him would be a purely physical event. Wrong. Almost inevitably, sex with the ex reawakens bittersweet emotions. Many a woman who's gone back for an encore returns with a haunted look in her eyes and a harrowing tale of sex conducted amidst huge wads of tear-stained Kleenex.

You might feel no emotion whatsoever. The only thing worse than tears is the hollow, slightly sickened feeling you get midway through sex when you suddenly realize you're making love with a man you don't care about, but nevertheless feel compelled to finish what you started.

Afterward, conversation might be strained, to say the least. You certainly won't be sleeping in late the next morning and reading the paper together the way you used to. More likely, you—or the dumpee—will immediately slink off in order to avoid any kind of conversation about what's just happened.

Your little tryst won't remain secret for long. If someone doesn't spot you emerging from his home at 7:15 A.M., rest assured that the dumpee will tell a few friends where you spent the night.

You might feel ashamed of yourself. In fact, if you have any moral fiber at all, you will feel, as Esther puts it, "like a waste of a human being."

In short, an encore is far more trouble than it's worth. Oh, and we almost forgot: it's terribly unfair to the dumpee. Now, many a dumpee will say just the opposite, and swear up and down that he would welcome the chance for a sexual reunion. "When you get ditched, you feel like you'll never get laid again," explains Tom. "It's like, 'Oh God, now I have to go out and look for a new job.' So if the woman comes back offering sex, of course you're grateful."

But beware: chances are very good that the dumpee still cares about you, and he'll view sex as

THE DEVIL
MADE ME DO IT

Backsliding is always preceded by sinful thoughts. In fact, if you go back for an encore, you are probably guilty of at least one of the seven deadly sins.

LUST

After dumping a Sexual Savant, it's not uncommon to experience an urge to sample his wares again. This desire can recur long after you've found a partner who's superior in every respect—except one. You know it's crazy, but you can't stop replaying your steamy memories of the Sexual Savant. Finally, you decide that there's only one way to put a stop to this nonsense: see him in person, at which point you'll realize that you're well out of the relationship. So you dash over to his house in the middle of the night, wearing nothing at all underneath your raincoat, telling yourself, "I'm just going to drop by to say hello. I won't even stay long enough to take off my coat."

ANGER

Post-ditch, it may so happen that you set your sights on a new man and are inexplicably rejected. You feel hurt—and enraged: how dare he? Well, you'll show him! Men will be lining up around the block to spend time with you! Why, there's already one man who definitely finds you irresistible: the dumpee. In fact, you're going to totter over to his house right now and magnanimously allow him to have his way with you.

COVETOUSNESS

Shortly after you've broken up, your ex begins trotting around town with another woman. You're not threatened by her in the slightest, but you hate the idea of anyone else staking a claim to *your* dumpee. Your reaction is like that of a child who has lost interest in a toy: as soon as someone else wants to play with it, it seems infinitely more appealing. But you're an adult, so you do the mature thing. You don't snatch him back—you sleep with him instead.

SLOTH

The dumpee turns up at your door one evening, carrying on about how he'll never love anyone else, and seems disinclined to leave. You just can't be bothered to deliver the whole breakup sermon all over again, and besides, you need your beauty sleep. So you let him spend the night. You might be tempted to justify this as an act of mercy—*it would have pushed him over the edge if I'd rejected him*—but in reality, you were simply too lazy to kick him out.

PRIDE

After a preemptive strike, in which you were forced to dump him lest he dump you first, you're plagued by a nagging doubt: was he less than enthusiastic about the relationship because he didn't find you sexually appealing? You decide to settle the matter once and for all: after a crash diet, you squeeze yourself into the tightest outfit you can find and invite the dumpee out for "a friendly dinner," where you proceed to flirt with him so relentlessly that he has no choice but to sleep with you.

GLUTTONY

Meaning, of course, both excessive eating *and* drinking. A time may come, post-ditch, when you have put on a few pounds and are feeling rather low; then, you bump into the dumpee, who says, "You look great! Have you lost weight?" Naturally, you wind up sleeping with him. Alternatively, there may come an evening when you have tied a few on and place a maudlin phone call to the dumpee, who quickly divines that you're temporarily minus your critical faculties, and rushes over to "help put you to bed."

ENVY

Three months or so post-ditch, the joys of single life are wearing a bit thin. The sight of a couple strolling down the street, hand-in-hand, evokes a potent mixture of resentment and longing: why does everyone else in the world have someone, except you? Which is when you succumb to the urge to hunt down your dumpee.

Regardless of your motive, the wages of sin are the same: the dumpee is brimming with happiness—he thinks you're back together—and you have to ditch him all over again.

an indication that you've changed your mind about the breakup.

If you can't be swayed by appeals to your conscience, however, perhaps appeals to your self-interest will do the trick. Raising your dumpee's hopes only to dash them all over again doesn't make others think well of you. In the wake of your breakup, all might seem calm, but in fact, a public relations battle is being waged—and it's crucial that you don't give your enemies any ammunition. Read on.

CHAPTER THIRTEEN

Spin Control
How to Position Yourself as The Bigger Person

S ome relationship experts will tell you that breaking up is a private matter, and advise you to maintain a decorous silence about the causes, nature, and aftereffects of the rupture. We have a little more respect for your intelligence. We assume you know that breaking up is a highly public act, and that the longer the two of you have been together, the more public it will be.

If your relationship lasted more than six months, ending it may prompt a referendum on your character. Everyone will have a theory: "She's so ambitious, and he just isn't a climber," or "She was getting mighty cozy with Antoine toward the end," or "It wasn't exactly *her* decision."

You can't stop people from talking, but you *can*

The Image You're Trying to Create

Really good spin ensures that post-ditch, your reputation is intact, if not enhanced. Your aim is to appear dignified, mature, and highly eligible. To achieve these lofty goals, you must emphasize that:

You dumped *him*. No one should think for even an instant that you were ditched. It is one of the inalterable laws of physics that a dumpee's social status plummets immediately post-ditch, whereas a ditcher's soars, particularly if she's rejected a guy who's seen as a catch.

You're not cocky. If onlookers think that the ditch has gone to your head, there's likely to be a backlash—followed by a surge of support for the downtrodden dumpee.

You are a gentle dropper. Your manners are impeccable, your methods unimpeachable, and you treat your dumpees as humanely as possible.

You are bravely struggling through a difficult time. Elated as you might be to have rid yourself of the dumpee, you must affect the demeanor of a woman who looks fabulous, yes, but is mourning a terrible loss. Otherwise, you risk seeming callous, and anyone who is inclined to take sides will run to the dumpee's camp. But don't overdo the performance, lest you discourage would-be suitors.

influence what they say. Never forget the first rule of public relations: perception is reality. In other words, how you actually treated the dumpee is less important than the way you are *perceived* to have treated him.

A CRASH COURSE IN SPIN CONTROL: TEN RULES TO LIVE BY

1. EARLY TO SPIN, EARLY TO RISE

Do not wait until rumors are flying to begin spinning your breakup. Then, your only option will be damage control. Better to head off nasty gossip altogether by marketing your own version of events right away.

2. SOLIDIFY YOUR BASE BEFORE WOOING UNDECIDED VOTERS

The first people to call are your staunchest supporters, most of whom will take your side automatically. But you can actually motivate them to go forth and spin on your behalf if you give them a sense of *ownership* over your breakup.

Consider inviting a few of your most zealous boosters over for a post-ditch stakeout. The correct wording of the invitation is as follows: "Oh my God, I just broke up with Fred—you'd better get over here right away!" If the phone rings after they arrive, shriek, "Don't get it! It's him! He keeps calling and saying he wants to get back together." After you've served the hors d'oeuvres, make a big production of pulling all the shades, as though lovesick Fred might be outside at this very moment, screwing up his courage to beg for one last chance. This evening will be such an intense bonding experience that the participants will remember your breakup as a glittering social event.

Winning over the mutual friends is a little trickier. Lest the dumpee get to them before you do, don't wait more than a day to call and say, "Fred and I broke up yesterday. He really needs your support right now, so I'd consider it a personal favor if you'd phone him. By the way, any chance we could have dinner this week? My treat." That way, if he carps about what an uncaring, selfish person you are, they'll have prima facie evidence to the contrary.

3. The best defense is a good offense

Shaping public opinion means anticipating change, not just reacting to it. You should be prepared to spin events even before they occur. For instance, if you suspect your dumpee is about to take up with a new woman, thus giving others the impression that he's over you, this is your cue to spin: "I think he's finally getting the message that I've moved on."

4. Don't bad-mouth the dumpee

Never openly slander your dumpee. Although

negative campaigning can be effective, the practitioner invariably looks nasty, ruthless, and desperate. So even if he and his cohorts are bad-mouthing you, don't retaliate. Simply say, "Fred is a wonderful guy," or, if that would strain credulity, "I prefer to honor our history with silence."

In a breakup, The Bigger Person is the one who appears to be the most respectful and generous toward the other. If you seem to be above the fray—and seem not to care about the outcome—you will win the public relations war.

Of course, none of this means that you can't *insinuate* all kinds of sinister things about the dumpee. Take advantage of every opportunity to make Sphinx-like pronouncements about other people's relationships, because your remarks will inevitably be read as clues to your own situation. On hearing that another couple is having difficulties or is deliriously happy, sigh knowingly and declare, "No one ever *really* knows what goes on in anyone else's relationship," or, "Nothing between two people is ever as it seems."

Another good ploy: if necessary, drop carefully selected tidbits in a seemingly nonjudgmental fashion. For example, "Fred was very principled. Why, whenever anyone gave him a hard time about subscribing to *Big Jugs,* he would deliver the most passionate defense of the First Amendment—honestly, he sounded just like a lawyer!"

5. KISS (Keep It Simple, Stupid)

The key element of spin control is a simple tale with a gripping narrative and a few concrete examples. Abstractions like "This is a time in my life when my priorities are changing" won't do the trick. Your audience wants a human interest story, such as, "He wanted someone like his mother, who's very traditional—a slave, really." Once you come up with a good story line, repeat it shamelessly. If pressed for alternative explanations, simply launch into your story one more time: "See, the problem was really that he wanted someone like his mother . . ." After you've told it enough times, it will become the official version of events.

6. The best lies have a kernel of truth and a bushel of detail

If it's necessary to gild the lily when it comes to your own conduct, do so deftly. A wholesale fabrication is never as believable as an artful lie that contains a grain of truth and is bolstered by a raft of convincing, though wholly fictional, details.

For instance, if others suspect that you had an

affair behind your dumpee's back—a faux pas that, if proven, will make you Public Enemy #1—do not deny any acquaintance with the Other Man. Rather, say something like, "Yes, Antoine and I have been friends for a while. In fact, he helped me through that really rough time when my aunt was sick, remember?" Toss in as many details as possible about your aunt's illness—how she contracted it, the various remedies proposed by doctors—and once your listener's eyes have glazed over, say, "So that's how Antoine and I got to be friends. And it's been so magical these past few weeks, the way that friendship has just blossomed into something more."

7. Give them something *else* to talk about

The best way to get your breakup out of the headlines is to come up with a fresh story about someone else: a friend's affair, a colleague's pink slip. But failing that, you'll have to invent something about yourself—a setback at work, say, or a devastating betrayal by a childhood friend that no one else has met (or ever will meet, since she's a figment of your imagination).

If neither option seems dramatic enough to sideline your breakup, pick the war-torn country

SPIN OR LOSE

How to make yourself look good in a bad situation

THE TRUTH	THE SPIN
Your dumpee also happens to be your boss. While the two of you were dating, your coworkers were intimidated by your access to the throne of power and curried favor with you big-time. Now, they're trying to distance themselves.	Hint broadly that they owe you their jobs. For example, "You know, Sue, Mr. Boss used to have this crazy idea that you were a total incompetent. Well, you can bet I set him straight on that one." You may want to suggest that the breakup has a certain temporary quality about it—and if you take the boss back, you'll remember the little people.
You briefly dated (and, okay, fooled around with) a man you now realize is a world-class embarrassment—and he's telling anyone who will listen.	Affect airy amusement: "Is *that* what he's saying? That's what I liked about him . . . (pause for effect) his vivid imagination."
You've started seeing another guy within hours of bidding your dumpee adieu.	Discretion is the watchword: frequent out-of-the-way bistros, or, better yet, invest in a few candles and a red-check tablecloth, and convert your own bedroom into a bistro. Refrain from raving to others about the wild nights you're enjoying.

THE TRUTH	THE SPIN
You've started seeing another guy within hours of bidding your dumpee adieu—and it's the talk of the town.	Issue an all-points bulletin: "Yes, I've met someone new, but we're taking it slow. I'm still not over Fred." Two weeks later, allow your friends to convince you that *you* shouldn't be afraid of commitment just because things didn't work out with Fred.
One of the dumpee's friends is bad-mouthing you.	Do not confront the friend, who is clearly spoiling for a fight. Instead, say, "That guy is so obsessed with me! He's acting like I broke up with *him*."
Your mutual friends have taken sides, and you're out in the cold.	Call a few ex-friends and tell them: "I just want to say how much I appreciate the fact that you aren't taking sides," which might shame them into welcoming you back into the fold.
You fear that others will figure out that you executed a preemptive strike ditch, and that your claim to the exalted status of ditcher is suspect.	Invent a new love interest: "I had to get rid of Fred because I was falling in love with Antoine." Next, add a few layers of mystery to generate a buzz: purchase two striking floral arrangements and display them prominently, telling all who ask, "I don't know who sent them, there was no card. I would guess Fred, or Antoine—or maybe both."

of the month and claim to be worried sick about your foster child there. When anyone calls, be sure that CNN is blaring in the background, and respond to all inquiries about the breakup by snapping, "How could I possibly talk about something so trivial when my foster child is going through such unspeakable horrors?" Overnight, you can transform your public image from that of a witch who broke the heart of the nicest guy in the world to that of a big-hearted, serious-minded girl who's dogged by tragedy.

8. IF YOU CAN'T CLAIM INNOCENCE, CONFESS—THEN CLAIM VICTIMIZATION

If you know beyond a shadow of a doubt that some damning information is about to be revealed, you have no choice but to break the news yourself, immediately. Remember the spin doctors' rule of thumb: confess what is likely to become known, deny what is likely to remain unknown, and spew out everything you've decided to say in one sitting, preferably accompanied by tears. Volunteering a salacious detail or two that isn't already floating around out there is a good idea—it makes it seem as though you're coming completely clean.

Establishing your credibility is crucial, since it

will almost certainly be necessary to imply negative things about the dumpee to save your own skin. For example, "I really liked Fred, but he was a little controlling. After a while, it seemed that the only way I could assert my independence was to sleep with dozens of other men. It's weird—once you're out of an unhealthy relationship, you look back and you can hardly believe some of the things you did just to *survive*."

9. Never let them see you spin

People don't like to think they're being manipulated, so it's very important to simulate sincerity. Your listeners should feel that they have to pry information out of you, an impression that's easy to create if you make liberal use of two stock phrases: "This is very hard for me to say," or, "I couldn't tell this to anyone else, but . . ." Your tone should be hesitant, your facial expression pained, and your arms crossed, as though you are determined to carry the secrets of this relationship to your grave.

10. The spin doesn't end when you start dating again

It is customary on a first or second date to have a brief discussion about past relationships. More than likely, your new suitors will have done some research, so don't pretend that you're a woman without a past. But be careful what you say, because it will be analyzed very closely.

First, the new man will want to know how recently your last relationship ended, to determine whether you're on the rebound. You can allay this fear immediately by saying, "We *formally* broke up just eight days ago, but in reality, the relationship was over long before that. We were just going through the motions."

Second, he'll be trying to divine clues about how you'll treat *him* from what you say about the dumpee. So be charitable. For example, "There's still a sense of loss. He was—I mean, he *is*—a really nice person." It's critically important to praise your ex, not only because it establishes your own generosity of spirit, but because it lays the groundwork for dumping his would-be replacement, should you have to, with the exit line: "I thought I was ready for a relationship, but I was wrong. I haven't recovered from the last one."

CHAPTER FOURTEEN

The Aftershocks

I f the relationship with the dumpee was at all serious, brace yourself for the aftershocks. Some will occur during the first few days post-ditch, but others might not be felt for weeks or even months.

A BRIEF PERIOD OF HYSTERIA (HIS)

There is often a week or two of craziness after the breakup, when you're fielding calls from the dumpee, sometimes in the wee hours. Perhaps he's bitter and needs to fling accusations at you. Maybe he's weepy and just needs to hear your voice. He might even be highly melodramatic: "I'll never be with another woman if I can't be with you." Whatever his modality, such calls are not cause for alarm—if he needs to vent, let him—and they should stop after a few weeks.

If they do not, and he starts turning up at your home or place of work or threatening you in any way, you are not dealing with a besotted dumpee but with a stalker. In which case, put down this book and call the police.

Breaking a second heart (your mother's)

If you're under the age of thirty, telling your mother that you've dumped a guy isn't so difficult. In fact, she may very well be elated.

After your thirtieth birthday, however, it's possible that your mother will be even more upset than the dumpee. She may question your judgment—"Are you sure you've thought this through?"—or demand a full accounting: "And what was wrong with *this* one? Well, if you weren't sure you wanted to marry him, why on earth were you leading the poor man on?" She might even go into her trademark faux introspective mode and murmur, "I guess it's too much to hope that I'll live long enough to see a grandchild." And that may not be all. Don't be surprised if, years down the road, you're complaining about some guy or other and your mother pipes up with, "What did I tell you? You should have stayed with Fred."

Now, you *could* simply neglect to mention the breakup to her. But if you live in the same country as your mother, this is risky: the average mother has a bloodhound's nose for changes in her daughter's romantic situation.

Or you could tell her that *he* dumped *you*. But that strategy, too, has a downside. She might feel compelled to offer you a little motherly advice, like, "Maybe if you'd put on a little makeup once in a while, this wouldn't have happened," or, "I could tell from Day One that he never really cared about you, but I didn't say anything because I knew you'd get angry."

The third option is the one we advise: tell your mother that you got rid of the dumpee because he said he was living for the day when he could ship his parents off to a nursing home. We assure you that she'll applaud your excellent judgment.

POSTPARTUM DEPRESSION (YOURS)

During the weeks immediately preceding and following your breakup, you are center stage: friends are calling constantly to get status reports, there are ongoing dramas with the dumpee, and everyone seems interested in knowing what's going on in your life.

Then, suddenly, calm. Dead calm. So calm that

no one even bothers to ask anymore about the breakup. It's already ancient history.

You're surprised by how empty you feel. For quite a while there, the breakup dominated your life, and now that it's over, you're not quite sure what to do with yourself. Aside from missing the limelight, you might also find yourself missing the dumpee—not so much that you regret ditching him, but enough that you're feeling rather sorry for yourself. And then, just when you think you've hit rock bottom, you hear that he's dating up a storm. It doesn't lift your spirits any.

Meanwhile, despite the fact that everyone you know has been saying for weeks that they'll fix you up "with a great guy," not one guy, great or otherwise, has materialized. Your calls to remind your friends of their promises yield less than satisfactory results. One tries to stall you with vague talk of a party she's planning to throw at some point in the distant future: "It'll be easier for both of you if I don't fix you up directly—that would be too much pressure." Another says, "Who? Oh *that* guy! Funny you should ask—he hooked up with a really sweet woman just two weeks ago, and they're already talking marriage." A third says, "You know, I've thought about it, and I don't think he's right for you. He only dates models." You've stopped speaking to a fourth, because she did finally produce a guy: the biggest geek you've ever laid eyes on. Your melancholy deepens.

Not to worry. A brief period of depression is to be expected post-ditch, and it will almost certainly pass on its own, without the help of psychotropic drugs.[1] And when it does, one of two things will happen: you will discover that you're happier on your own, or that your newfound sense of well-being makes you a magnet for men.

Neither a borrower nor a lender be

If your ex is at all eligible, it is possible that an acquaintance might approach you with a request: "Since you're not interested, would you mind if I went out with him?" Instantly, your hackles rise: there's a predator in your midst.

But then you calm down and think about it for a minute. Why *shouldn't* she have a crack at him?

---

[1] During this difficult time, you might toy with the idea of consulting a psychiatrist. Save your pennies: the only thing worse than post-ditch depression is shelling out $120 an hour to sit in a stuffy office and prattle on about all the terrible things that happened in your childhood. Your money would be better spent at the aesthetician's office, where at least you get some immediate results.

Besides, you can't imagine what the dumpee would see in *her*. So you reply, "Of course I don't mind!"

Now, if you only dated the man a few times and have absolutely no interest in him, it's probably the right thing to do (although you shouldn't be in a big hurry to introduce any new boyfriends to this particular "friend"). But in all other cases, allowing someone else to rummage through your romantic castoffs is a very bad idea.

If the dumpee doesn't like her, she might very well resent and envy you—what did you have that she doesn't? And if he does like her, *you'll* feel envious and resentful—was he secretly lusting after her the entire time you were going out? Worse, if they remain in your social orbit, you'll be forced to make nice with the happy couple.

There are two ways to avoid these messy complications. First, be alert to the signs that you're dealing with a would-be poacher. Generally, before requesting your blessing, she asks a few leading questions: "So, is it really over?" Or, "Is there any possibility you two might get back together?" You must act swiftly and decisively. Reply, "You know, there *is* a possibility we might get back together. Definitely." It's not even a lie. But she doesn't need to know that the possibility is one in a million.

Alternatively, you can wait until she actually comes right out and tells you she has designs on your dumpee, then smile sweetly and say, "I don't think that would be good for our friendship." Of course, she may go right ahead and do what she wants anyway, but at least you'll ensure that she feels a twinge of guilt.

You, on the other hand, should feel no guilt whatsoever about standing in the way of other people's happiness. If the dumpee and your "friend" are really meant to be together, they will be. In fact, you will have done them a favor: their love for each other will be that much stronger because they've had to surmount some obstacles.

Oh, by the way, if you're considering dating one of _his_ friends, let us help you think this decision through: don't.

REVERSAL OF FORTUNE

A year after the breakup, your dumpee has made a complete recovery. He recently landed a high-profile, high-paying job, and your spies tell you that he's engaged to the beautiful brain surgeon you read about in _Vanity Fair_. You, however, are still living in a cramped basement apartment, scrounging money off your parents to pay the phone bill, and trying desperately to hang onto your on-again, off-again relationship with a guy who isn't even qualified to be the dumpee's gofer.

How could it be that just last year, you were riding high and the dumpee was pleading for one more chance? How could it be that your positions in the world have reversed so dramatically?

We don't understand it ourselves. But sadly, it's a fact of life that your dumpee might one day be wildly successful and/or rich and/or married, and you might be none of these things. The disparity could bring out an envious streak you didn't even know you had, and you could spend many wistful hours thinking that if only you hadn't dumped him, you'd be sharing the limelight with him this very minute.

But don't despair. Although there's really nothing you can do to change the situation, keep in mind that your fortunes, too, could change: there's a growing interest in tell-all memoirs penned by bitter ex-girlfriends.

CHAPTER FIFTEEN

How to Get Him Back

When You Realize You've Made a Horrible Mistake

Before you got rid of your dumpee, chances are good that you eagerly anticipated life without him: complete freedom, dates galore, doing whatever you wanted whenever you wanted. And perhaps the reality has lived up to your expectations. Perhaps you're happier now than you've been in years.

Or maybe everything was great for the first little while, but now life seems a bit colorless. The thought of yet another first date where you're forced to trot out the same old moth-eaten anecdotes makes you queasy. The prospect of another overwrought, soul-baring girls'-night-out fills you with ennui. Consequently, you seem to spend a great deal of time at home, alone, wondering how long it would take someone to discover your corpse if you died of boredom.

Sooner or later, a thought pops into your head, one so aberrant that you dismiss it immediately. But it creeps back: *maybe I made a mistake*. There was, after all, no compelling reason to ditch him. He's not only a Garden-Variety Man—he's a particularly fine specimen of the breed. The more you think about it, the more certain you become: the dumpee was the man for you. You must get him back!

Then it hits you: maybe he doesn't want *you* back. And who could blame him? You distinctly recall telling him that you were absolutely, one hundred percent certain that your relationship could never work.

And perhaps you were right. Maybe if you got back together, you'd be sick of him within the week. Or maybe, just maybe, you'd live happily ever after.

Even if it's clear to you that your renewed interest in the dumpee is, in fact, genuine, proceed with caution. You have to be absolutely certain. Dumping him once is acceptable, but double-ditching borders on cruelty.

You should also be aware that if he takes you

Perhaps you're just idealizing him—or maybe you really are meant for each other. So ask yourself

Do You Want Him Back Because...

1. You haven't had sex since ... well, you can't even remember when?
Yes_____ No_____

2. You're now willing to accept him as he is, flaws and all?
Yes_____ No_____

3. You're suffering from amnesia: you have no memory of ever finding him terribly irritating?
Yes_____ No_____

4. You've *really* changed (e.g., you got rid of the dumpee mainly because you weren't interested in a serious relationship, and now you know you are)?
Yes_____ No_____

5. Your whole life is a misery?
Yes_____ No_____

6. He's *really* changed (e.g., he used to be a teetotaler, and now he's loosened up considerably)?
Yes_____ No_____

7. Everyone you know is getting married?
Yes_____ No_____

8. You were on the rebound when you started dating—or he was—and the relationship never got a fair chance?
Yes_____ No_____

9. Your dumpee is showing every sign of being over you?
Yes_____ No_____

10. You can't stop thinking about him: "That shirt would look great on my dumpee," or, "I wish I could tell my dumpee what happened today—he's the only one who would understand"?
Yes_____ No_____

Questions 1,3,5,7,9: If you answered yes to more than one, refrain from begging him to take you back. You're suffering from self-pity, not regret.

Questions 2,4,6,8,10: If you answered yes to just one or two of these questions, sure, you miss the guy a little—but not enough to warrant a reunion. If you answered yes to three or four, your renewed interest might in fact be worth pursuing. But if you answered yes to all five, we question your veracity: you've really changed *and* he's really changed? A likely story.

back, you will still have to work very hard to repair the rift. He might find it difficult, if not impossible, to forgive you for dumping him; you might find it difficult, if not impossible, to hang your head and apologize, over and over and over. And you should be prepared for the fact that news of your reunion might not be greeted with joy by the dumpee's intimates, who have in all likelihood been slandering you for some time now.

There might be logistical obstacles, too, like the new girlfriend he's acquired. If your dumpee is at all honorable, he won't toss her aside just because you snap your fingers. In fact, he might already be quite fond of her.

But what's life without a challenge or two? Although no strategy for winning him back is foolproof, our sources report that the following are worth a shot.

THE SOCIAL AMBUSH

You arrange to bump into the dumpee accidentally-on-purpose, as often as possible, always looking your very best. You then proceed to flirt with him so subtly that if he's not interested, you can reasonably claim you were only trying to be nice and had no designs on him.

PRO: *Even if the dumpee doesn't take the bait, he might be more warmly disposed toward you.*

CON: *He might fail to respond because a) your technique is so indirect that he's not even aware you want him back, or b) he's recently discovered that he enjoys sex a whole lot more when he's having it with a woman who isn't quite so manipulative.*

Feigning illness

One pathological liar whose talents we respect immensely swears by this method. She pretends to have a medical problem—nothing too serious, but something that involves test results and a period of bed rest—and gets someone else to urge the dumpee to "help care for the invalid," which involves giving sponge baths and rubbing various ointments on her "feverish" body, which is clad only in a scanty teddy. The dumpee is usually so excited about performing these duties that he doesn't even notice the "patient's" temperature is exactly 98.6°F.

PRO: *Dumpee feels virile—he's responsible for a miraculous recovery.*

CON: *He insists on a doctor's note.*

THE REVERSE PSYCHOLOGY METHOD

The strategy here is to make the dumpee think it was *his* big idea to get back together. One way to accomplish this: call him up and say, "Have you come across one of my earrings? No? Well, I'm sure I lost it at your place. Can I come over and look?" Race over there in your shortest skirt, and when he quite naturally gawks at your half-naked body, say, "I do believe you're trying to seduce me!" If he denies it, just murmur, "Well, you must be doing it unconsciously. But let me tell you, it's working."

PRO: *Dumpee relishes sweetness of winning back the woman who ditched him.*

CON: *He realizes with horror that your cellulite is visible at thirty paces.*

APPOINT A MINISTER
OF PROPAGANDA

A favorite of the fainthearted. You enlist a mutual friend to try to broker a reunion with the dumpee. Generally, the friend is coached extremely carefully and charged with a specific mission: to tell him only those things that cast a flattering light on you. For example, "She's looking better than ever these days." Next, the friend tests the waters: "Do you ever think about getting back together? You know, I think she really misses you." If your Minister of Propaganda is amenable to accepting a bribe, consider requesting that the following sentence be uttered to the dumpee: "Did you hear that she was approached recently by a scout for a modeling agency?"

PRO: *Enables you to spread good news about yourself without looking egotistical.*

CON: *The friend might make a hash of the job—or the dumpee might say, "It's weird that you think so highly of my ex. She never had a good word to say about you."*

THE WOE-IS-ME APPROACH

Recommended only for accomplished liars. You embellish on a minor crisis to make it seem like a medium-size tragedy, then call on your ex for help. For instance, a vending machine eats your quarters, which gives you the idea to call him and say, "I've been mugged! They took everything I had! I'm scared out of my mind—could you come over?" This gives him the chance to feel like a white knight, and gives you the chance to turn to him with dewy eyes and exclaim, "I never could have gotten through this without you." As you thank him, kiss him, ever so tentatively, as if it's just now occurred to you that you want him back.

PRO: *Dumpee revels in new he-man image.*

CON: *He insists on enlisting professional help—e.g., "I'm calling the police, and we're filing a report right now!"*

TAKE BACK THE BREAKUP

You tell the dumpee that you were temporarily insane when you gave him the heave-ho, and cannot be held responsible for your own actions. "Remember how my back was killing me? The doctor prescribed some incredibly potent painkillers, but I didn't tell you because I didn't want you to worry. Well, sweetie, it turns out that the side effects included severe mood swings and depression! It was only when I finished the prescription that I realized how crazy those pills were making me. When I told you I wanted to break up, it was the drugs talking."

PRO: *Dumpee can save face—"The long and the short of it is, she was drugged to the gills when she ditched me, but she's clean now."*

CON: *He'll never let you have so much as an aspirin again—"I don't care how bad your cramps are! Remember what happened last time?"*

THE MEA CULPA

Honest, mature, and terribly risky. You tell the dumpee in a straightforward fashion that you are sorry you broke up with him and want very much to get back together: "I really miss you. I think breaking up was a huge mistake, and I want to apologize for it and for hurting you. Would you consider taking me back?"

PRO: *Has the charm of truth.*

CON: *Requires nerves of steel, a strong stomach—and a willingness to eat crow.*

One last note. It's been known to happen that a woman recaptures her dumpee's heart and, just when she believes they'll live happily ever after, finds herself on the receiving end of a revenge ditch. Which is why we urge you to think carefully before dumping a guy and even more carefully about getting back together again: what goes around, comes around.

CHAPTER SIXTEEN

In Parting...

Now that you've thought through every eventuality and possible repercussion, we hope you're feeling better prepared for the task that lies ahead. But, if not, take heart: we used to be cowards, too, yet we managed to overcome our fears and bite the bullet—and we lived to see another day. Granted, that day was most unpleasant, since we faced it alone: guilt-ridden, consumed by self-pity, and exiled from polite society.

But don't let that discourage you. No matter how bleak the world looks immediately post-ditch, two things are certain: matters *will* improve with time, and you *will* meet another man—maybe even one you want to hang on to. Nevertheless, there are no guarantees when it comes to romance, so keep this book handy. You may need it again soon.

APPENDIX

For Men Only

Men often ask us, "Is there any way to tell that a woman is going to ditch me?" Yes. In fact, there are a number of universal warning signs.

◆ At parties, she flirts blatantly with all your friends—but treats you like her brother

◆ She stops sleeping in the nude—and starts coming to bed dressed as though she's heading off on an Arctic trek: thick socks, sweatpants, huge T-shirts

◆ When you try to surprise her with a special romantic weekend, she says, "This is really *very* inconvenient for me."

◆ When she introduces you to other people, she seems none too eager to reveal the fact that you're her boyfriend

◆ She takes a sudden, intense interest in her appearance, and rushes out to buy a slew of body-hugging clothes—which, oddly enough, she wears only on her "girls' nights out," which are now occurring three times a week

◆ When you come back from a ten-day trip, she says, "Back already?"

◆ You found this book on her bedside table—and the worksheet was filled out

What should you do if she's preparing to bolt? Accept defeat gracefully. It's your best chance of getting her back—or your best chance of being remembered as a one-in-a-million dumpee.

WORKSHEET

YOUR NAME: _____

DUMPEE'S NAME: _____
          LAST   FIRST   MIDDLE INITIAL, IF KNOWN

DUMPEE'S TYPE
(e.g., Cling-on, Sexual Savant, etc.): _____

_____

RATE YOUR COWARDLINESS ON A SCALE OF 1–10
(ten being "absolutely petrified"): _____

LENGTH OF RELATIONSHIP: _____

DATE YOU FIRST REALIZED
YOU HAD TO DUMP HIM: _____
          MONTH   DAY   YEAR

TODAY'S DATE: _____
          MONTH   DAY   YEAR

REASONS YOU'VE WAITED SO LONG: _____

_____

_____

_____

REAL REASONS FOR BREAKUP
(attach a 2–3 page essay, if necessary): _____

_____

_____

_____

_____

_____

REASON YOU'LL GIVE DUMPEE
FOR THE BREAKUP:

_____

_____

REASON YOU'LL GIVE OTHERS
(need not be one of the above):

_____

_____

ESTIMATED DATE AND
TIME OF DITCH:
_____
                   MONTH   DAY   YEAR
BELONGINGS AND/OR CASH
TO BE RETRIEVED FROM DUMPEE:

_____

_____

DUMPEE'S BELONGINGS AND/OR
CASH TO BE RETURNED:
_____

BREAKUP METHOD
(e.g., phone, letter, in-person):
_____

LOCATION OF DITCH, IF IN-PERSON:
_____

BREAKUP OUTFIT
(including shoes, jewelery, and accessories):
_____

_____

_____

EXIT LINE:
_____

_____

_____

ACKNOWLEDGMENTS

Thanks to our families,
for teaching us the importance of compassion, generosity of spirit,
and sensitivity to the plight of others.

Thanks to all those who shared their expertise
in the field of ditching. You know who you are, and why we must
protect your anonymity. We are at liberty, however, to thank
Eli Attie, Jim Barry, Laura Blumenfeld, Rick Diamond, Liz Egan,
Serena French, Fiona Hart, Christopher Hitchens, Marina Jimenez,
Arthur Kaminsky, Dave McKenna, Lucia O'Sullivan,
and Esther Singer.

We are deeply grateful to Peter Workman,
the man who had the courage to finance this learned treatise,
and the entire team at Workman Publishing, especially
Ruth Sullivan, our Muse (and long-suffering editor).

If you don't like this book,
blame Mickey Kaus and Catherine Keri, without whose help it
could never have been completed. We cannot say enough good
things about them, or place too much blame on their shoulders.

Finally, a very special thank-you to Will Falk,
who good-naturedly put up with all kinds of nonsense
from both of us.

THE AUTHORS

KATE FILLION, author of *Lip Service:*
The Truth about Women's Darker Side in Love, Sex, and Friendship,
and ELLEN LADOWSKY, author of *Jacqueline Kennedy Onassis,*
have been friends ever since they realized that they'd both
ditched the same man. Collectively, they have
thirty years' experience of dumping guys.